HOW NOT TO FAIL
YOUR
DRIVING
TEST

HOW NOT TO FAIL
YOUR
DRIVING
TEST

JOHN MARCHMONT

BookEns
LIMITED

BookEns Limited
HOW NOT TO FAIL YOUR DRIVING TEST
by
John Marchmont TD. Dip DI.

ISBN 0–9540692–1–8

Cartoons by George Hollingworth

Typeset by BookEns Limited, Pedlars Lane, Therfield, Royston, Hertfordshire, SG8 9PX.
Printed and bound in Croatia by Zrinski

CONTENTS

THE AUTHOR

John Marchmont has for many years run his own successful driving school in Nottinghamshire.

A member of the Institute of Advanced Motorists for over 30 years, he holds the advanced driving certificates for cars, motorcycles, commercial vehicles and for trailer and caravan towing. One of his many activities has been coaching associate members of the local group of the Institute of Advanced Motorists, preparing to take their advanced driving test.

'He represents his Area Driving Instructors' Association on the local Road Safety Committee, and was for some years an RAC Registered Instructor before the RAC closed down their driver training section. He holds the Associated Examining Board's Diploma in Driving Instruction.

In addition to 25 years service in the Territorial Army, his many hobbies have included motor rallying, sailing, caravanning, gardening, wine making, and various activities related to driver education and safety.

THE AUTHOR

He has driven well over a million miles in various parts of the world, in a variety of Service and civilian vehicles, and admits that he is still learning.

He is the author of *The Caravanner's Handbook*, published by BookEns Ltd., Royston.

There are already a host of good books on 'Learning to Drive' and 'How to Pass Your Test', so why did I write this one?

Well, the others all give excellent advice on what you should do to get it right, quite clearly and in a straightforward manner. What is sometimes missing though, is WHY you should do what you are told to do, and what are the most common mistakes which cause learners to get it wrong.

Perhaps I have a misplaced sense of humour, but I find so many how-to-do-it books rather dry and po-faced. I have taken a rather more light-hearted look at a none-the-less serious subject. I have tried to emphasise not only how to do it, but particularly how Not to do it. Most of the common mistakes are here, most of the reasons for failure which you need to avoid. I sincerely hope it will help to keep on the straight and narrow path that great multitude of hopefuls – the learner drivers.

There are two categories of people in this book. Some are fictional, others are, alas, only too real. Their names have been changed, of course, but they are real people. Indeed, alive and well, and for all I know still terrorising innocent road users while blissfully unaware of their own bad driving habits.

Who is in which category is a confidence I propose to keep, to be revealed only to The Chief Examiner Himself, assuming, that is, that I finally make it to the great test centre beyond the pearly gates.

FOREWORD

I am often asked if I passed by driving test at the first attempt – most people assume I did because I've gone on to make a career from behind the wheel. I did manage to pass first time around, and felt it was a terrific achievement. However, I'm occasionally tempted to go a little over the top and strut about like a peacock when telling this to people, by adding he words 'yes, and only a month after my 17th birthday, as well'

I've never given in to that boastful temptation through because I grew up in the shadow of my father who, as a teenage racing driver, passed his driving test on the very same day he turned 17. and his children aren't allowed to forget that family fact in a hurry!

But whether it's a day, a month, six months or years after your 17th birthday, it is a fantastic feeling to rip up your L-plates. You are allowed to be proud and, just for one day, you're allowed to be a little bit smug too, satisfied in the knowledge that all the hard work you and your instructor have put in over many lessons, has paid off. Big time.

FOREWORD

Not everyone passes at the first attempt though. And I'd like to stress that this doesn't make you any less of a driver. Far from it – I know plenty of racing drivers who needed more than one go before they were deemed fit enough to tackle the roads on their own. So if you have a test or two under your belt already, don't panic. Whether you're a first timer, or not-such-a-first-timer, you've done the sensible thing in wanting to learn more by picking up this book.

How Not To Fail Your Driving Test is a thorough guide to every step you need to make in order to achieve that highly desired prize – your driving licence.

The book covers all aspects of life on the road, from urging you to learn your highway code (which can actually be fun, honestly), to choosing the right instructor, getting to grips with clutch control, how to use speed correctly, and, finally, how to tackle the big day

Treat this book like a second driving instructor – one that won't charge by the hour and won't mind being questioned at all hours when clarification is needed on a driving point. Or two.

Along the way, *How Not To Fail Your Driving Test* tells little tales of how things can go wrong, which not only spieces up the serious issue of driving, but also helps you by highlighting how not to fall into similar traps.

All that's left for me to do is to hope that you all go on to enjoy driving as much as I do, and when it comes to your test, I wish each and everyone of you the very best of luck.

Vicki Butler-Henderson

ACKNOWLEDGEMENTS

I am most grateful for the considerable help and friendly advice given to me by Mr John Alexander.

There are few people in this country who know more about the complex subject of driver training and testing than John; his entire working life was spent in this field. He held a variety of senior appointments within the Department of Transport and prior to retirement his last position was that of Chief Instructor at the Department's Examiners' Training Establishment at Cardington.

John spent much time ploughing through my manuscript, with a nod of approval here and a tearing into shreds there. Without his encouragement and expert advice, the book would never have got off the ground, and I am much indebted to him.

I must also acknowledge the two groups who have been the source of most of the material in this book – my fellow motorists and my varied host of pupils.

I have cited the bad behaviour of a variety of idiots, but of course, not all drivers are like that. Many motorists take pride in their driving skill, and are worth observing.

And the pupils – ah, the pupils. Each one is memorable in one way or another. Without the ever varied range of triumph and despair, tears and laughs which I have shared with them, this book would certainly never have got off the ground.

It is, therefore, with no little affection and gratitude that I dedicate this book to that colourful, infuriating and gratifying assembly – my pupils.

INTRODUCTION

I am an expert on failing the driving test! There are now 22 main headings or sections under which the test can be failed, and over the years pupils of mine have come unstuck on most of them.

This book is a bit different from the usual driving books. For a start it is not essentially about learning to drive although it contains a lot of learning-related material. It is not so much about **passing** the test as about high-lighting and avoiding the most common reasons for test **failure**, and I have tried to do this in a cheerful manner.

We look at the best way to go about learning to drive. We look at driving instructors and we look at driving examiners. We look in detail at what the test actually requires of you, and we look at the test itself. Assuming you pass your test, we look at where you go from there, since passing the test is not the end of the road, only the beginning.

We are, of course, looking largely at the practical driving part of the test. In July 1996 the Government introduced the theory test, a simple multiple choice paper with some 35 questions. This test must be passed, in addition to the more recent Hazard Perception test and, of course, the practical test, before a full driving licence can be issued, and we look briefly at the theory test later in the book, plus the hazard perception test.

Finally, in these ludicrous days of political correctness, let me warn you that I do not propose to keep writing him/her or his/hers. Whether in praise or criticism I assure you I intend no sexual bias, so when you come to a pronoun, you can choose any gender you prefer.

Driving a motor vehicle is a very, very serious and responsible business, but it can also be a lot of fun. I hope you learn something useful from this book, and have a smile or two in the process.

DEPARTMENT FOR TRANSPORT BOOKS

To a brand new learner driver whose motoring knowledge probably goes little further than how to open the car door, a book about the test might seem a little premature, but read on ... The Department for Transport publishes three books which are essential reading for the learner driver.

The Driving Test is available from all good bookshops, and you should get a copy as soon as you have decided to learn to drive. It is very well laid out and illustrated. It tells you about instructors and examiners, and how to go about taking lessons. It tells you about the test itself and clearly lists the points the examiner is looking for. It goes through the steps to take after you have passed and even advises on what to do if you fail.

At one time a small book called *Your Driving Test* was sent free with every provisional driving licence. This was much less detailed than the current updated version. Sadly, people try to learn on the cheap and many will not part with the modest cost. I would encourage you to pay up – the money will be well spent.

The second book, *The Driving Manual* makes little or no reference to the test, but covers the whole subject of driving, way beyond the test, in a clear and comprehensive manner. It starts with a basic explanation of the controls of a vehicle and explains the function of things like brakes, clutch, steering wheel and gears. Basic exercises like moving off and stopping are covered, and then driving in traffic, dealing with junctions, roundabouts and other hazards. Simple law, night driving, bad weather driving, motorway driving, dealing with breakdowns, vehicle security, towing a caravan, driving abroad – this book is not just for the learner, it is every driver's bible. If every 'experienced' know-all with 25 years' bad habits behind him were to buy a copy of *The*

Driving Manual and do a chapter a night, then believe me we should soon stop killing over 3,000 road users every year. It is indeed a book for every driver, but it is an absolute must for the student driver.

The Driving Manual is applicable to all the 30 million drivers who share our crowded roads, and as such deserves much more publicity than it actually gets.

Finally – *The Highway Code*. This is not just recommended reading, **it is an absolute must for every driver**, and it deserves a short chapter by itself. We'll look at *The Highway Code* in more detail later.

Before leaving the subject of books we should just mention the theory test.

This book deals principally with your practical driving test, but since July 1996 all learner drivers have also been required to pass a theory test, and in this connection we must mention an absolutely indispensable book.

From The Stationery Office again, *The Complete Theory Test for Cars and Motorcycles* is a must. It deals in excellent detail with the form the test takes, the subjects covered, how to apply – in short everything you need to know.

If the theory test is taken when you are well into your course of practical driving lessons, you will already have acquired the experience to answer many of the questions. Your instructor should also be able to supply you with sample question papers, so that you can have a number of 'dummy runs'.

The Complete Theory Test is also available as a CD-ROM, which is extremely helpful and good value.

The theory and hazard perception tests are dealt with in more detail on pages 163 and 164.

THE HIGHWAY CODE

The current edition has been enlarged to cover all subjects included in the theory test, and is of such vital importance to the new driver as to deserve a chapter of its own.

It is the absolute authority on the rules of the road. It's cheap (around £1.50). It is clearly and simply written. It is well illustrated. It depicts every traffic sign and road marking you are ever likely to come across. It clearly lays down who does what, who goes first, and who gives way in almost every traffic situation imaginable. It caters for the vehicle driver, the motorcyclist, the cyclist, the pedestrian, the motorway driver – every road user in fact, and you must learn it.

Understand this:– if you don't know *The Highway Code* inside out, you will stand no chance whatsoever of passing either your theory or your practical driving test. So get one when you apply for your provisional licence, and read it, again, and again and again.

All too often beginners chuck it to the back of a drawer, intending to swot it up a few days before the theory test. This is absolutely, completely **wrong**. Leaving aside the sections for pedestrians and cyclists, there are almost 200 rules governing the actions of drivers, and well over 100 different traffic signs and road markings to learn. Your driving instructor is not going to teach you all these – that's your job; that's why you need the book right at the beginning. If you don't become familiar with the common traffic signs and the more basic rules of the road at the very beginning of your driving course, how on earth are you going to drive yourself and your instructor safely on the public roads?

I insist on my pupils knowing *The Highway Code* thoroughly within the first few weeks of starting their driving course. It is the yardstick by which all mistakes are recognised and corrected.

If you don't know *The Highway Code* inside out, you will stand no chance whatsoever of passing either your theory or your practical driving test.

I said 'leaving aside the sections for pedestrians and cyclists' but in fact that's wrong. Don't leave them out, read them. Get to know how the other half lives. Get to know what a pedestrian, a cyclist and a horserider could be expected to do under various circumstances. In other words, put yourself in the other road user's shoes. You are going to have to quite a lot of this. It is called ANTICIPATION.

Reading and understanding the Code early on in your driving course will make your instructor's explanation much easier to understand. You will come to realise that this is not just a lot of rules for the sake of having rules, it all boils down to common sense. We shall see that expression used a lot as we go through this book. Good driving is really no more than a mixture of good manners and common sense, and *The Highway Code* is based firmly on both.

While dealing with the written word rather than illustrations, don't overlook the section at the end, 'Road User and the Law'. Every road user needs this knowledge, learner or otherwise.

As for the pictorial bit, road markings and traffic signs, yes the road markings do take some learning, but they really are important, quite vital in fact, for road safety in general. The road signs, however, tend to be mostly obvious and self-explanatory. However, some can be misinterpreted Here are a few examples that are capable of an alternative meaning.

Both the following signs obviously refer to cycles but have quite different meanings. Do you know the difference between:–

this   and   this

  ?

Can you identify this? A lot of drivers can't. If you can't, go and look it up right away!

The visual, or pictorial content of *The Highway Code* is better illustrated in a little book called *Know your Traffic Signs*. It's published by The Stationery Office, costs very little and is available from any good book shop. The traffic signs and road markings are larger and clearer than in *The Highway Code*.

Do learn your stopping distances at various speeds, and get to know what these distances actually look like on the ground. There is no point in knowing that you need 36 metres to pull up in at 40 miles per hour unless you know what 36 metres really looks like. This knowledge is essential if you are to follow behind another vehicle at a safe distance.

Hand signals are shown in *The Highway Code*. Both these and stopping distances can also crop up in your theory test.

DRIVING INSTRUCTORS

A fairly reliable way to fail the test is to do your learning the very cheapest way you can.

This is certainly not a complete Do-It-Yourself book on learning to drive.I am assuming you are doing the sensible thing, and being taught by an authorised, professional driving instructor. Nothing less will do.

In this chapter, then, we'll consider **your instructor**.

If I wanted any offspring of mine to learn to fly an aircraft, go deep-sea diving or hang-gliding, I would try to find the very best instruction available. Yet when learning to drive on the public roads among over 24 million other vehicles, people fail to realise that this is probably the most dangerous activity they will ever indulge in.

Many learners therefore get Uncle Fred to teach them. Uncle Fred has no doubt driven confidently for 20 years or more, but it is highly likely that the last time he saw a Highway Code was when he took his test. Since then it is most unlikely that he has done anything to correct his accumulated bad habits or update his knowledge of the current rules of the game.

Uncle Fred also lacks the benefit of dual controls in his car and he is certainly not accustomed to taking corrective action from the passenger seat. (Yanking on the hand brake will achieve little apart from stalling the engine and starting a rear-wheel skid).

Another important gap in his qualifications will be a lack of knowledge about what the examiner will be looking for. He won't know about the 22 specific sections of the test and he won't have read *The Driving Test* in which they are covered in detail. He will also have little knowledge of the likely local test routes, and knowing them certainly helps. When he thinks you are about ready to take the test, could Uncle Fred put you through a realistic dress rehearsal? Does he know enough about the way the test is conducted to give you an exact replica of the experience, i.e. a mock test? A professional instructor should give you several mock tests, word-for-word and step-by-step just like the real thing. Nothing prepares you so well for the actual day as a couple of realistic dummy runs. Only an ADI (Approved Driving Instructor) has the knowledge and experience to do this. Without these dummy runs, test day itself remains for you an enormous question mark, and you are unprepared for taking it easily in your stride. You can in fact do just that if you have been properly prepared beforehand.

Finally, Uncle Fred might be a good and capable driver, but lacking in the techniques of instruction. Conversely he might be a good, patient and steely-nerved instructor, but with poor knowledge of up-to-date road safety procedures.

A professional driving instructor must have passed stiff exams in road safety, both theoretical and practical driving, and in the techniques of teaching every aspect of driving. In addition to these initial qualifications, he is re-examined regularly by Department for Transport Supervising Examiners in order to retain his instructor's licence.

So, a professional driving instructor must by law be an ADI, that is an Approved Driving Instructor, registered with the Driving Standards Agency (of the Department for Transport). He or she must display on the car the licence to teach. This carries his name, photograph and ADI's registered number. There is an illustration of such a licence in the new edition of *The Driving Test*.

Alternatively he could be a trainee instructor, holding a trainee's licence, and working under the supervision of a qualified ADI. In this case the car will display a triangular licence, coloured pink. A trainee instructor will have passed some of the qualifying exams, but not all. A trainee's licence is only valid for six months, after which the final qualifying ADI exams must be taken.

Anyone who gives driving instruction for financial or other reward who does not hold an ADI's or trainee instructor's licence is breaking the law, and the penalties are heavy.

So, find a good professional instructor. Don't be too much influenced by persuasive adverts. Preferably get a personal recommendation from someone who has been well taught by a local school.

Don't shop around for the cheapest. In this field, as in many others, you usually get what you pay for.

A keen and conscientious instructor who is anxious to build a good business and a reliable reputation will usually go to some trouble and expense to gain further qualifications over and above his basic ADI's licence. He will probably be a member of one of the professional bodies such as the Driving Instructors' Association (DIA), or the Motor Schools Association (MSA). He will more than likely be a member of the Institute of Advanced Motorists (IAM), may have taken the Royal Automobile Club (RAC) instructor's test and become an RAC Registered Instructor. A more recently qualified instructor will not be on the RAC register; unfortunately the RAC have now closed down their register of instructors, but driving school cars with RAC 'L' plates are still to be seen. An instructor may also hold a Diploma In Driving Instruction (Dip DI). This is a high qualification run jointly by the Driving Instructors' Association and the Associated Examining Board, and involves five separate examinations.

The ultimate goal for a driving instructor is to hold the Diamond qualification, which involves passing a very demanding driving test devised and supervised by the Department for Transport, and conducted at their Examiner Training Establishment in Bedfordshire.

Incidentally we have already mentioned that the part of the Department for Transport which is responsible for matters relating to driver training and testing was re-named the Driving Standards Agency during the Spring of 1990. To avoid confusion we will, from this point on, refer to the Driving Standards Agency (the DSA).

In addition to the qualifications already listed, an instructor might well become qualified to teach disabled drivers. This is a very specialised skill, and anyone who has need of such tuition should contact the local Area Traffic Office, which will be able to give details of a suitably qualified instructor.

If you go for the cheapest lessons you can find you will, as we said, get what you pay for and very little more. The instructor concerned will probably not have a very good opinion of his services or he would not be charging such a low fee. It could be that he is not particularly successful and somewhat desperate for business.

So, do find a really good instructor; it's a wise investment for the future. The higher the standard of your instruction, the better driver you will become, and obviously you will reach this standard more quickly.

DRIVING TEST EXAMINERS

Driving test examiners fall into the same category as the rent man, mother-in-law, tax inspector and traffic warden. They are often the butt of caustic humour and wild rumours, most of which are completely unfounded and near-libellous.

Contrary to popular belief the examiner does not have matted hair on the back of his hands, one eye in the centre of his forehead or blood-stained fangs. Neither is he some benevolent old bumbler who will automatically pass you if you are wearing a mini-skirt, (particularly if you're a feller).

Examiners are human and subject to human whims and frailties. They do a basically boring but difficult job, are subject to the same pressures as other folk, and a great deal more than many. They run considerable risk of personal injury and most of them can recount some hair-raising experiences. There is a recorded instance of an examiner on test actually being driven into a canal by the candidate.

If you turn up for your test in the dual-controlled modern car of a reputable driving school, your examiner will obviously feel happier at the prospect of you driving him in this vehicle, than in Uncle Fred's ten-year-old banger with two torn L plates tied on with string. In theory it will not affect the outcome of the test at all. You are judged solely on your driving performance, not the appearance of the vehicle, or whether or not you have a severe case of bad breath. However, the driving school car tells the examiner two things before you even set off. One is that you have been presented for test by a responsible, professional instructor who would not let you attempt the test unless you had, in his view, reached pass standard.

The second thing is that in the event of your getting out of your depth at any time, he – the examiner – has dual controls to fall back on. He is going to greet you, therefore, with a less jaundiced eye than he would have done in Uncle Fred's old banger.

The Driving Standards Agency trains examiners (for cars, motorcycles, LGVs, PCVs etc.) on a thorough and rigorous course at Cardington, in Bedfordshire. The examiners' own personal driving skills are brought up to a very high level, and a rigid standard of uniformity is instilled into their assessment of driving faults in others.

It is the Department's proud boast that examiners are passed out from Cardington like peas in a pod, so that exactly the same assessment of a test drive would be given, whether performed in Aberdeen or Exeter.

Of this idealistic pronouncement one has to be a little sceptical. It's a fine theory, but not very practical. We have said that examiners are only human. Individual humans, with widely varying temperaments. Some are cheerful, jolly characters, kind to children, animals and old ladies. Others are exceedingly miserable from the moment they get out of bed, as are many atomic scientists, milkmen, bank managers or any other collective group. Even, believe it or not, driving instructors.

Examiners are intelligent individuals with individual powers of judgement and initiative, so despite the training, they will inevitably occasionally place their own personal construction on events. So one will put more significance on handbrake, another on mirror, and so on.

Indeed, at one test centre, we had an examiner who rebuked an instructor because his pupils were pulling up at the kerb without giving the appropriate signal, regardless of the fact that there was no other road user in sight. Within ten days, another examiner had rebuked the same instructor because his pupils were now giving 'unnecessary signals'. Officially it's impossible, in practice it's inevitable.

Examiners, like instructors, are regularly monitored and checked by a Supervising Examiner, who will visit a test centre at random, and ride in the back of the vehicle during tests. This is not done to observe the candidate so much as the examiner. Examiners whose standards of assessment are out of line with the norm are soon taken to task and 'straightened out' by their supervisors.

That excellent book *The Driving Test* tells you in question and answer form at the beginning of the book, quite a lot about the way the test is conducted, and about what the examiner is likely to say. In fact he does not say very much at all. He is not there to encourage, support or sympathise with you. Nor will he criticise you during the course of the test. He is there simply to observe and judge your ability to cope, on your own, with whatever circumstances you might meet.

He knows only too well that you are feeling nervous and apprehensive, and he will make allowances for this. It is part of his training to greet you in a cheerful and friendly manner, and to do his best to put you at your ease.

Despite earlier comments about there inevitably being some difference between individual examiners, they really are trained to a high level of professionalism and uniformity. No matter where you take your test, the procedure is exactly the same, and a good instructor is able to give you a sound insight into the examiner's routine and the manner in which the test is conducted.

One could write a separate book about examiners, and I'm quite sure that most examiners could write a fairly penetrating volume about instructors.

In the interests of simplicity we refer to examiners as 'he', but by no means are all examiners male. There are indeed lady examiners and we could not write a chapter about examiners without a passing reference to Mrs Whitbread. If the DSA's elite Corps of Examiners were to have its own version of the SAS, this force would inevitably be led by Mrs Whitbread.

A powerfully constructed lady, Mrs Whitbread stood no nonsense from candidates, instructors or indeed from other examiners. She had reddish, frizzy hair of a texture similar to the pad your Mum uses for shifting burnt custard from the saucepan. Never what you would call a snappy dresser, she mostly appeared in a longish, shapeless tweed skirt which was topped by a knitted garment, reminiscent in style and cut of the uniform of a Chinese railway official.

When downwind of her, one could sometimes catch the tantalising fragrance of Owbridges Celebrated Cough Mixture. When on the move, if a luckless candidate were to brake too sharply, Mrs W. would permit herself to lurch forward in her seat belt and click her tongue disapprovingly for several seconds. This did very little to improve the candidate's morale.

Sitting in the dentist's type atmosphere of the test centre waiting room, we instructors would speculate on the origins and circumstances of Mrs Whitbread. Was there a Mr. Whitbread, we wondered? We pondered on the nature and form of this hapless individual. Was he allowed to drive the family car under the laser beam of her beady eye? We shall never know.

She was not with us for long. No doubt it was felt in high places that her particular talents were wasted in our quiet little market town. She was probably despatched to put the fear of God into other, more truculent candidates, perhaps in some riot-torn suburb of one of the larger, rougher cities.

ABOUT THE TEST

For 50 years or so the British driving test remained virtually unaltered, but with our increasing involvement in the European Community there are bound to be changes in the future.

In 1990 a proposed new syllabus for driver training was devised which goes much further than the simple standards of the test which is still in use today. This syllabus takes up three pages at the end of *The Driving Test* and glancing through it you can see that it is a much more comprehensive programme of learning than the one which is currently taught. One day, this syllabus will be the basis for our British test, but for now we use the form of test which has been in use for so many years, with a few amendments plus, of course, the theory test and hazard perception test.

In 1996, coinciding with the introduction of the theory test, *The Highway Code* questions were dropped, and replaced by 'knowledge of the ancillary controls of the vehicle'. This now fills the last section of the current marking sheet.

Let's now get one important item straight; a fault during the test does not automatically mean failure. There is a great deal of wrong information put about in this connection, and your instructor can give you the facts, which are as follows.

There are three types of fault which an examiner can record:

a. a minor fault, or driving fault
b. a **potentially** dangerous fault (a "serious" or major fault)
c. an actually dangerous fault (also a major fault)

ONE instance of either b or c during the test drive means failure, but minor faults (a) do not, UNLESS you incur more than a fixed number of minor faults. This number is currently 15, but may be reduced in the future. It could be however that if you committed the same minor fault several times, the examiner could consider such repetition to be a major fault.

The definition of a minor fault? Well, it's not easy to define and may well differ according to the circumstances and the examiner's interpretation, but generally a minor fault is one in which no other road user (including pedestrians) is involved, inconvenienced or endangered. An example might be failing to check handbrake and 'neutral' before starting the engine. If the gear was in fact in neutral, no harm done – a minor fault. If the car were in gear, starting the engine could cause it to jerk forward. Any pedestrian crossing the road in front of the vehicle is immediately in danger, and you clearly have a major fault.

Since 1993 a copy of the examiner's marking sheet (form DL25c) is given to every candidate – pass or fail. Previously the candidate who passed did not receive a copy of the examiner's sheet, only the 'pass' certificate, so those who passed never knew what minor faults had been committed.

Another helpful step forward in the test procedure is that the examiner will offer to explain verbally to a candidate who fails, exactly what driving error has been responsible for failure.

Not all wish to discuss it. Some are so distraught, incredulous, furious, tear-stained or plain gobsmacked that they don't want to hear about it. It is a great improvement, however, that this explanation is there to be had. For very many years, despite urgent pleas from instructors' organisations, examiners were forbidden to discuss the result of a test with either the candidate or the instructor. This was always a grossly unsatisfactory business and, fortunately, is now in the past.

So let's get down to looking at the 22 sections of the test.

THE 22 SECTIONS OF THE TEST

The following is a list of the 22 sections of the test. Any fault committed during the test will be marked under one of these headings. As you see, some of them are divided into sub-sections.

1. **Comply with the requirements of the eyesight test**

2. **Take proper precautions before starting the engine**

3. **Make proper use of**
    a. accelerator   b. clutch
    c. gears   d. footbrake
    e. handbrake   f. steering

4. **Move away**
    a. safely   b. under control

5. **Stop the vehicle in an emergency**
    a. promptly   b. under control

6. **Reverse into a limited opening to the right or left**
    a. under control   b. with proper observation

7. **Turn round using forward and reverse gears**
    a. under control   b. with proper observation

8. **Reverse park**
    a. under control   b. with proper observation

9. **Make effective use of mirror(s)/ rear observation well before**
    a. signalling   b. changing direction
    c. changing speed

10. **Give signals**
    a. where necessary   b. correctly
    c. properly timed

11. **(A) Take appropriate action on all**
    a. traffic signs   b. road markings
    c. traffic lights
    (B) Take appropriate action on all signals by
    a. traffic controllers   b. other road users

12. **Exercise proper care in the use of speed**

13. **Keep a safe distance behind vehicles**

14. **Make progress by driving at a speed appropriate to the road and traffic conditions, avoiding undue hesitancy**

15. **Act properly at road junctions with regard to**
    a. speed on approach   b. observation
    c. position before turning left   d. position before turning right
    e. cutting right hand corners

16. **Deal with other vehicles safely when**
    a. overtaking   b. meeting
    c. crossing their path

17. **Position the vehicle correctly during normal driving; exercise lane discipline**

18. **Allow adequate clearance to stationary vehicles/obstructions**

19. **Take appropriate action at pedestrian crossings**

20. **Select a safe place for normal stops**

21. **Show awareness and anticipation of the actions of other road users**

22. **Use of ancillary controls**

Starting on page 28 we will take these 26 headings and see just what each one actually means. *The Driving Test* takes these sections one-by-one and tells you what the examiner expects you to do.

DECLARATION

I declare that my use of the test vehicle for the purposes of the test is covered by a valid policy of insurance which satisfies the requirements of the relevant legislation. Signed...

E Jones

Driving Test Report

Candidate's Name: EDWARD L. JONES

Vehicle Type: Peugeot 306

Registration No.: FD 51 XPJ

Driver Number: J O N E S 8 1 2 2 3 4 E L 5 A D

Safety Questions		S	D			S	D
1(a). Eyesight				12. Use of speed			
1(b). Highway Code (Categories F/G/H)				13. Following distance	1	1	
2. Precautions				14. Maintain progress by :-			
3. Control :- accelerator				driving at an appropriate speed			
clutch	1	1		avoiding undue hesitation			
gears				15. Junctions :- approach speed			
footbrake				observation			
handbrake	1·1	2		turning right			
steering				turning left			
balance m/c				cutting corners			
4. Move away :- safely				16. Judgement when :- overtaking			
under control				meeting traffic			
5. Emergency stop :- promptness				crossing traffic		1	
control				17. Positioning :- normal driving			
making proper use of front brake (m/c)				lane discipline			
6. Reverse to left or right :- control				18. Clearance to obstructions			
observation	✓			19. Pedestrian crossings			
7. Turn in the road / control				20. Position for normal stops			
'U' turn (m/c) :- observation	✓	1	1	21. Awareness and planning			
8. Reverse parking :- control				22. Ancillary controls			
observation	R C						
9. Use of mirrors / rear observation (m/c) well before :-							
signalling							
changing direction							
changing speed							

Visitor: [ ]   Total driving faults :- 0 6

10. Give appropriate signals :-				23. Result of test	Pass	Fail ✓	None
where necessary	1	1					
correctly							
properly timed							

Route number: 4

Examiner's signature: *T Welling*

Examiner's name: D. WELLING.

11. Response to signs and signals :-	
traffic signs	
road markings	
traffic lights	
traffic controllers	
other road users	

Extended test		1	3
		2	4

Supervision SDE [ ] SE [ ] AOM [ ] ACDE [ ]

Test Terminated in the Interest of Public Safety		Pass certificate No.		ADI Number	7 6 8 7 4	Category
Test Terminated at Request of Candidate				Test Centre	H A W T O N	
Examiner Took Action	Verbal ✓	Physical	Staff number	Date	0 3 1 0 4	M ✓
Oral Explanation Given	Yes ✓	No		Time of Test	1 1 4 1	F

DL25C   DSA - An executive agency of the Department for Transport, local Government and the Regions   2/03
© Crown Copyright 2002

This book aims to show you how **not** to fail your driving test, so what we shall do is look at these 22 headings and go carefully through what you should **not** do. In other words we will look at the faults candidates often commit which cause them to fail under these various headings, and consider how to avoid them.

Above shows the examiner's marking sheet, by kind permission of the Driving Standards Agency.

Pass or fail, the examiner will give you a copy of the marking sheet so that you can see where you committed any fault, which the examiner will be quite happy to discuss with you.

You could, of course, complete your test with no faults at all, even minor ones. This is by no means uncommon, and if you can get through with a clean sheet, you have reason to be well pleased with yourself.

The marking sheet shown represents a fictitious test of a fictitious candidate by a fictitious examiner.

Edward Jones had comparatively few minor faults – two on use of handbrake and one on use of clutch, missing out a signal, not enough all round observation on the turn in the road, and a bit of following behind another vehicle a little too closely.

What failed him was a dangerous incident when crossing the path of another vehicle. He was probably turning right without due consideration for an oncoming vehicle. The examiner has marked the box indicating that he took physical action, obviously by making use of the dual control brake and clutch. He has marked the section 16 box in the 'D' column indicating that the candidate's action was actually dangerous.

SECTION 1 OF THE TEST

The eyesight test

You must be able to read a vehicle number plate at a distance of 20.5 metres (22 yards or 66 feet), where the numbers and letters are 7.5 cms (3 inches) high.

After you have met your examiner at the test centre, and 'signed in', and he has taken a look at your provisional driving licence and your Theory Test pass certificate, you will both walk out to the car but before getting in, the examiner will say something like 'will you please read the number plate on the red car on the other side of the road?'

If you have to screw up your face and say 'what red car?' you have rather blown it. Usually you will be asked to read the number from a greater distance than the prescribed 20.5 metres, and if you have difficulty in doing so, then you will be asked to move a little nearer. If you are still unable to read the number the examiner will return to his office for a long measuring tape, and the exact distance from the car will be measured out.

If you cannot read the numbers from this point then the test is terminated and you have failed. You can bring letters from doctors, eye specialists, opticians or whoever, but you still fail, and there's no way round it. That is the standard eyesight test, no more, no less. You may of course wear spectacles or contact lenses, but if these are worn for the eyesight test they must be worn for the practical driving part of the test.

As a yardstick for a vehicle driver's vision the whole charade is inappropriate, inadequate and bordering on the ridiculous. You might have one glass eye, tunnel vision, double vision, colour blindness or a dozen other optical defects, but if you can read a number plate at 20.5 metres you're in, and if you can't then you are out.

Many influential bodies who are closely connected with road safety have repeatedly expressed concern over this matter, but it remains unaltered. In recent years a Minister of Transport has actually been quoted as saying that he could see no connection between drivers' defective vision and road traffic accidents. In the face of this sort of overwhelming logic, it seems likely that the present practice will continue.

Safety Questions

In the interests of the safe operating of vehicles, the DSA introduced, in 2003, a small addition to the driving test, in which a candidate's practical knowledge is tested.

Immediately after the eyesight test the examiner will ask two questions relating to day-to-day vehicle maintenance. There are about twenty possible questions, such as 'How do you check the level in the windscreen washer reservoir?' or 'How do you check the air pressure in the tyres?' or 'How do you check that the indicators are working?'

You could be requested to 'show me how …' or 'tell me how …'. In the case of 'show me how', e.g. checking the level of brake fluid, if your demonstration necessitates opening the car bonnet, your instructor is allowed to open the bonnet for you, but no more.

Your instructor will have shown you where to locate the radiator water tank, the brake fluid reservoir, the windscreen washer reservoir, etc. If you are not sure of where anything is, or what the tyre pressure should be for example, don't hesitate to say 'I would first check in the car's handbook', because all these routine maintenance tasks are fully described in the handbook.

If you answer one or both of these questions incorrectly you only earn a minor fault. This is not a pass or fail item, although a minor fault here counts towards the final total of minors.

To stop life getting too heavy, a little light relief can creep into almost any situation. A colleague of mine recently reported an examiner asking one of his pupils 'how do you check the level of oil in the engine?'

'Pull out the dipstick and check the oil level on the stick – it should be between the two marks' replied the pupil.

'Right', said the examiner, 'and if the level is low, where do you put extra oil in?'

A brief pause. 'At the garage', she replied.

I'm told the examiner smiled, and that's got to be a plus.

SECTION 2 OF THE TEST

Precautions before starting the engine

Whenever you get into your instructor's car I hope you run through the drill which the examiner will want to see before you set off on your test drive.

Make sure the doors are closed, adjust your seat and mirrors correctly and put on your seat belt. You should also demonstrate to the examiner that the driver's head restraint, if fitted, is at the correct height. Right, now to start the engine. Check handbrake on, gear lever in neutral, operate the starter. A simple, almost automatic routine.

Suppose though that you had operated the starter with the gear lever in 1st gear and the handbrake not on very firmly. If you tried to start up in this way, the car would leap forward, probably bashing into the car in front, or breaking both legs of the little old lady who had decided at that moment to cross the road in front of you. So you always check handbrake and neutral first. Easy enough in a relaxed but attentive mood. What about this simple routine when under pressure though? Just see what happened to one of my pupils on a mock test.

We were stationary at traffic lights, the first vehicle in the queue. Immediately behind stood a vast menacing articulated lorry, his radiator grille a metre or so from our rear window. The driver was revving his 8 litre engine to advise us that as soon as the lights turner amber, never mind green, he was going to be away. The other ominous factor in this scenario – we were on a slight uphill slope.

In my role as examiner (a mock test, remember) I sat silently. The lights changed, and Sally, the pupil, now thoroughly intimidated by the knight of the road astern and anxious to escape him, brought her clutch up too sharply and stalled the engine. A stifled sob escaped followed by a very rude word. Desperate to escape she turned the ignition key, but we were still in gear with the clutch engaged and the handbrake off. My long-suffering car leapt forward and stalled again.

Had this been a normal lesson, I would now have come to Sally's rescue, calmed her down and reassured her. This was not a normal lesson however, this was her second mock test, a taste of the real thing. I continued to look out of the window therefore, wearing the glazed look of po-faced detachment which all examiners strive for. Again she stalled through rushing the clutch, and again tried to restart with the engine in gear. The lights had changed back to red by now and the 'artic' had moved in to within inches, engine bellowing. I took pity on Sally and talked her through the procedure and out of an uncomfortable situation.

We had a post mortem discussion at the end of her mock test, with the pupil looking depressed and wretched.

We highlighted the fact that had this been her actual test, she would not necessarily have failed just for stalling, but would certainly have done so for trying to restart the engine without going through the handbrake and neutral drill. She agreed that she had, in desperation, lost her grip on the situation, and would not have earned a licence to drive by herself.

One can at times restart the engine while still in first gear, provided the clutch is disengaged. On this occasion that would not have been appropriate since we were on a slight slope, and with no handbrake, we would have rolled back.

So, as the book says, take proper precautions before starting the engine. Easy enough at the start of a routine lesson or in a quiet side street. Would you still get it right under pressure, with the large 'artic' right behind you? Do remember this small but very important point – it's a pretty silly way to fail your test.

SECTION 3 OF THE TEST

Proper use of the accelerator, clutch, gears, footbrake, handbrake, steering

If you turn back to page 24 where we list the 22 sections of the test, you might notice that the first 10 sections are all to do with the physical control of the car. Nothing to do with coping with traffic or dealing with other people, just your actual control of the vehicle.

Following the eyesight test and precautions before starting the engine, actual car management starts here in section 3 of the test schedule, with the main controls.

There are six major controls on a car, three hand controls and three foot controls, and they are listed at the top of this page. Two facts need to be accepted concerning the operation of these six controls:

1. It is frequently necessary to operate two or even more of the six controls at the same time; and
2. Unless you are dealing with an emergency stop, **all** the controls need to be operated smoothly and gently.

Accelerator
Let's take the six in order then, and start with the 'go faster' pedal, or 'gas' pedal, which is less of a mouthful than 'accelerator'. It has less up and down movement than the other two pedals, probably only moving through a distance of about 7.5 cms. Those 7.5 cms, however, depending on which gear you are in, can represent the

difference between 20 mph and 100 mph, so the pedal obviously needs treating with care.

The most common faults to avoid are (a) not enough gas pedal, (b) too much gas pedal and (c) stabbing the foot on and off the pedal too abruptly.

Not enough gas pedal is a very common fault, particularly when moving away. It stops (or 'stalls') the engine because, by using the clutch, we have connected up to the engine the dead weight of the stationary car and passengers, without the engine having enough power, or momentum, to get them moving. In this situation the weight of the load stops the engine, all for want of a bit of gas. If the revolving engine is going to move the stationary car, that engine must have some momentum behind it; in other words it must be going at a reasonable speed when it is actually connected up to the loaded car.

Beginners often stall this way through fear. Fear of the car leaping away out of control if too much gas is used. OK, a very reasonable reaction, but it is basically wrong. You must have faith in the fact that the speed at which a car moves away has very little to do with how fast the engine is going. How fast you move away really depends on how fast you connect up the car to the engine, in other words, how fast you connect up the clutch, and we'll deal with the clutch in the next section.

Now for too much gas; apart from occasions when it is a simple case of travelling too fast, too much accelerator usually happens when you are travelling so slowly that it is necessary to have the clutch partly disconnected. (This means that the two clutch plates are slipping on each other, and we'll discuss this when we look in detail at the clutch.) When a slipping clutch is needed you are probably doing a reversing manoeuvre, or some task that calls for the car to be moving very slowly. Doing this, learners often have the engine turning much too fast, with the gas pedal pressed too far down. The engine makes an awful lot of noise, there is excessive use of petrol and a lot of unnecessary exhaust fumes.

The excessive engine noise tells you immediately that you are using too much gas pedal, and the examiner will mark a fault under this heading.

Jabbing the accelerator and lifting off it too sharply will give a very uncomfortable ride, particularly if the car is being driven in a low gear. This is because the lower the gear the more rapidly the car will respond to an increase or decrease in gas, because the lower the gear, the more power is produced. A learner in the early stages often experiences this kangaroo hopping effect. It

When you move away, increase the engine speed with the gas pedal gently. As the clutch begins to bite and the car starts to move, continue to both increase the gas and connect up the clutch – both of them gently. You'll never stall if you do this.

sometimes occurs on moving off. If the gas pedal is pressed too hard, the car responds and leaps ahead. Result – panic. Foot lifted sharply off the gas pedal, car slows down rapidly, almost as if the brakes had been applied hard. Your passenger is therefore thrown forward, having just previously been hurled backward when the car leapt ahead. It only happens in the lower gears but is most unpleasant and alarming. **Gently** with the feet.

If you want to convince your passenger that you know what you're about, there's nothing to beat moving off and gaining speed smoothly. **Never** stab the accelerator, squeeze it gently.

Doing two or more things at once calls for a deal of concentration and coordination, sometimes more coordination than the learner is capable of. Some people have better coordination than others, and these are the pupils who make better progress during the early stages of learning to control the vehicle. It isn't easy to concentrate on bringing one foot gently up whilst squeezing the other one down, at the same time looking where you are going. Practice and more practice is the answer and remember, use your accelerator foot **gently**.

Clutch

I once had a middle aged lady as a pupil who had left it rather late in life before learning to drive. On our first lesson we were parked in a quiet country lane, and I was about to go through the basic drill, and explain the controls and their functions. She got in first however.

'Now Mr Marchmont' she said briskly 'don't even think of telling me what goes on under there' – pointing to the bonnet – 'I shouldn't understand it and I'm not interested, I simply want to be able to get to Sainsbury's.'

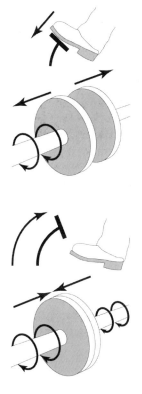

Now I don't work that way and I hope your instructor doesn't either. I showed this lady a very simple drawing of the clutch mechanism and explained how the engine drove one half of the clutch and the other half was connected to the rest of the car. When the two halves of the clutch were connected up, the engine moved the car. You disconnected the clutch by pressing the pedal down and connected it by letting the pedal come up. She thought this was brilliant and very helpful, and in no time at all was moving away really smoothly, thanks to having some understanding of what the clutch did and how it worked.

The commonest error among learners is to imagine that there are only two positions for the clutch pedal – up or down. Think of these as 'black' and 'white' and then you must realise that there are many shades of grey when using the clutch. There are many occasions when it is necessary to have the two halves of the clutch only partly connected to each other. The two round, flat plates are not pushed tight up to each other so that they are both revolving at the same speed, they are held fractionally apart so that one is going round faster than the other, in other words they are slipping on each other. This is the 'slipping clutch' we spoke of in the accelerator section, and it is used when you wish to creep along very slowly.

When you move away you MUST connect the clutch plates gently; bring them to the point where they are just beginning to 'bite' on each other, at which point the car begins to move, very slowly. Now it's at this point that beginners tend to stall the engine. They think 'right, we've cracked it', and they whip the left foot straight off the clutch pedal. This bangs the two clutch plates together, with one of them revolving and the other one still virtually stationary. The result is that the stationary one, with all the weight of the car attached, drags the other one to a rapid standstill, thus stopping, or 'stalling' the engine.

We mentioned under 'The Accelerator' heading that when moving away, you must bring the clutch up until you feel it begin to bite, then gently add more gas and gently bring the clutch the rest of the way up. Allow the car to cover 10 metres or so whilst you are connecting up the clutch, don't try to do it all of a rush.

Perhaps the clutch fault which examiners see most frequently is known as 'riding the clutch'. This involves coasting along with the clutch pedal pressed down, in other words with the two clutch plates disconnected. Two common examples of this fault are (a) when approaching a stop, the pupil presses the clutch before beginning to apply the brakes, and 'freewheels', often for a considerable distance before actually braking.

The correct way to deal with stopping, which of course occurs frequently, is as follows. Plan well in advance the place where you wish to stop and begin by lifting smoothly off the gas pedal; with less fuel supplied to it, the engine will slow down. Because the engine is still connected to the road wheels, the whole car will slow down. If the clutch is pressed on the other hand, the engine will be disconnected from the rest of the vehicle, and is unable to exert any braking or slowing down effect. The car therefore just rolls on under its own momentum. To stop correctly therefore, lift off the gas pedal first, apply gentle brake and as the car slows down, disconnect the clutch just before you stop. **Don't press the clutch first**, this will certainly earn you a fault.

The other frequent instance of riding the clutch is on cornering at a junction. Imagine a left turn into a side road A learner will frequently do all the approach procedure correctly, mirror, signal left, check the position of the vehicle for the turn, brake gently, speed down, change into second gear on approaching the corner and then they spoil the whole thing by keeping the clutch pressed down while they 'freewheel' round the corner.

The moral is, if you have selected the correct gear for any particular task, for Heaven's sake connect up the clutch and use that gear. The reason beginners get it wrong here is, once again, fear. Fear of going round the corner too fast. You see, a learner tends to associate the act of connecting up the clutch with moving away and gaining speed, and he doesn't want to gain speed just as he's approaching a corner. It's the very moment when he wants to have everything under control. I can tell you that you haven't got everything under control if you are freewheeling. You don't have the braking effect of the engine, which we were talking about just now. I can promise that if you change down into a 'go more slowly' gear and re-connect the clutch, you will do just that, you will go more slowly. That is unless you are pressing the gas pedal, but you don't do that as you approach a corner; your foot should be covering the brake, not the gas pedal.

So don't ride the clutch and do connect it up **gently**. Press it down as fast as you like, but for a smooth ride, bring it up **slowly** and **smoothly**.

Gears

Few things will damage a vehicle more than persistently driving in the wrong gear for the speed at which you are travelling. The gear you choose for any particular task depends on the speed at which you intend to carry out the task.

This might be the right moment to consider one of my favourite definitions of good driving. It means:

Speed dictates the choice of gear.

1. being in the right place on the road at the right time;
2. travelling at the right speed for the circumstances;
3. being in the right gear for that speed.

If you look into any traffic accident it is likely that someone had got one of these three points wrong. In fact if you are not doing all three of these things all the time, you are probably committing a test-failure fault.

What is the right gear for the speed? Well, most learners know that on level ground, any speed over 40–45 mph is dealt with in 5th gear, right up to the British maximum 70 mph.

What is often overlooked is the fact that the other four forward gears only deal with fairly narrow bands of speed, each speed band extending over about 10 mph. So, the right gear for the speed looks a bit like this:–

standstill up to 10 mph	1st gear
10 mph – up to 20 mph	2nd gear
20 mph – up to 30 mph	3rd gear
30 mph (approx) upwards	4th gear
40–45 mph upwards	5th gear

The above figures are only a guide, and will vary from car to car. Note, however, that the higher the gear you are using, the wider the range of speed you can achieve in that gear.

These speed bands do overlap each other, but not by much, so in a town situation (30 mph) any drop in speed of 10 mph or more means you almost certainly need to change to a lower gear. Often the learner who has not developed a sympathy with the car and the engine will allow the car to drag on at a speed which is too low for the gear. This puts a damaging load on the engine, which can be heard 'labouring' i.e. turning over far too slowly. Your instructor will demonstrate this to you early in your course.

Do remember then, if you have to reduce speed, consider whether you need to change down to a lower gear. If you are bowling along out of town doing, say, 65 mph and you have to reduce speed to 45 mph, then your top gear will continue to be appropriate. However, any reduction in speed below 40 mph will almost certainly need a gear change.

Another gear-related fault which is so easy to slip into is the tendency to come to a stop and forget to change into 1st gear before moving off again. Roundabouts are often the cause; you reduce speed on approaching a roundabout, often changing into 2nd in the hope of entering the roundabout without having to stop. At the last moment a vehicle approaches from your right, so it's change to plan B and stop. As soon as a suitable gap appears you start to move off, only to find that you are still in 2nd, the gear you arrived in. Trying to move off in any gear except 1st will almost inevitably mean you struggle forward a metre or so and stall. So there you are, nose sticking out onto the roundabout, a dead engine, egg on face and a great artic coming straight at you from the right. **FAIL!**

The moral here is: every single time you stop, you either go 'hand brake on and into neutral' (depending on how long long you think you will be stationary) or change straight into 1st gear, ready for the move off.

Get into the habit of doing this, otherwise you will find yourself over and over again trying to move off in the gear you arrived in. It doesn't work.

We've dealt with remembering to change down when you slow down. The opposite of this is equally important. So often I have seen in lessons or mock tests, a pupil will slow down and change into 2nd gear before turning into a side road, then speed up but proceed to travel the whole length of the side road, still in 2nd gear. A certain 'gear fault' to an examiner. First and second gears are for driving very slowly for whatever reason, and they are also for building up enough speed to get up into a 'cruising' gear when traffic permits. No way, though, is 2nd a 'cruising' gear. However, 3rd certainly is, although obviously not on a straight clear road. In a town or on a housing estate however, where 30 mph is a bit too fast, 3rd can often be a cruising gear. Too often learners will accelerate away from a hazard, be it a junction or whatever, and fail to change up into a cruising gear. They whirl along doing nearly 30 mph, still in 2nd, with the engine turning over at a furious pace, obviously crying out for a higher gear. Quite a common cause of test failure, and so unnecessary.

We have just used the word 'hazard', and we shall see it again quite often. Let's just consider what a hazard consists of. A hazard is anything which causes you to either slow down, alter course, or both. So a junction, a roundabout, the Gas Board's hole in the road, a parked car, a suicidal pedestrian, all these are hazards. All hazards need the same treatment. You think about and act, if necessary, on these five items, always in this order:-

1. Mirror
2. Signal
3. Position (of your vehicle)
4. Speed (slow down)
5. Gear (change down)

MIRROR SIGNAL POSITION SPEED GEAR
(Must Surely Prevent Some Grief)

If you always deal with these five items in that order you will always arrive at your hazard in the correct place on the road at the right time, at the correct speed and in the correct gear.

> Every single time you stop, you either go 'hand brake on and into neutral' (depending on how long you think you will be stationary) or change straight into 1st gear, ready for the move off.

> Remember – if you're travelling at the right speed for the traffic and road conditions and you're in the right gear for that speed, you won't go far wrong.

41

Finally let me warn you about two little habits which are so easy to get into but not nearly so easy to break, and either of them could result in you failing your test.

1. **DON'T** look down at your gear lever when changing gear. You know the position of each gear, relative to the others, or you certainly should do. Mark out a big letter 'H' on a piece of paper. Number the positions of the gears, add on an extension for reverse, and 5th, look at your drawing and **LEARN IT**.

   Get your instructor to let you sit in the car, engine running, clutch pressed down, and practise finding all the gears, in any random order. When you are driving and need to change gear, you'll find the gear lever is just where you left it after the last change. You should be able to drop your left hand straight onto the gear lever without taking your eyes off the road. It's also essential to know which gear you are in at all times, otherwise how do you know which way to move the gear lever during the next change, or even where to find the lever without looking down? Try to master this right at the start of your course. Looking down, as we have said, is a bad habit to get into and quite a common cause of test failure.

   I remember an examiner who was a wise old owl stressing this point to a pupil. He pointed down to the gear lever and said 'nothing has changed down here', then pointed to the windscreen and said 'up here things are changing all the time – which one should you be looking at?'

2. The second little potential fail habit is all too common. Don't drive along holding the gear lever. Your father has probably done it for years, but don't you start. Between gear changes, put your left hand back on the steering wheel. The gear lever won't fall off if left alone, so don't keep hold of the thing just because you might do another gear change further down the road. Believe me, this is a frequent and really silly way to fail the test.

Footbrake

When you need to slow the car down, the first thing is to lift your foot off the accelerator pedal. This will always slow you down (unless you are going down a steep hill). If lifting off the gas doesn't slow you down enough then you use some footbrake. The handbrake is not used to either slow down or stop, and we'll deal with this in the next section. If you need to come to a complete stop, then you certainly need the footbrake, lifting off the gas will only slow you down – you won't stop altogether.

There are four common faults under this section:–

1. Braking too late   } these two usually go together.
2. Braking too hard
3. Braking too soon
4. Braking too gently

Numbers 1 and 2 are the usual reason for the examiner marking a braking fault. If you approach a T junction, or any 'give way' or stop situation and you are approaching too fast, then your braking will have to be concentrated in the last few yards. When a vehicle stops with the brakes applied hard, the nose of the car dips down and driver and passenger are thrown forward in their seat belts as the car stops. Braking as hard as this is the result of not bringing the speed down earlier, in other words, not anticipating the need to stop in X metres. Apart from an emergency situation, the need to brake hard almost invariably results from braking too late, and will earn you a major fault.

Fault number 3, braking too soon, results in your running out of steam before you get to the hazard which is causing you to brake, and so coming to rest too soon.

Fault number 4 is equally simple. Braking too gently means that you will over-run the point at which you wanted to stop, i.e. you bash into the car in front, which has already stopped. If you were not intending to stop but just slow down, then too little brake pressure simply means you won't slow down as much as you had intended. Number 4 is very easily remedied, just squeeze the brake pedal a little harder – it's as easy as that.

Now all this must seem totally obvious to most people, but please don't think I'm talking down to you. A considerable number of learners have problems with braking, so I want to spell this out. One very common problem is stopping too soon. There is a red traffic light so we must stop. Right, apply the footbrake and be ready to press the clutch just before we stop. OK so far. Now we sit and watch, horrified, as the car slows down and down and is obviously going to stop completely, long before we get anywhere near the place where we intended to stop. Embarrassing to say the least.

This running out of steam too soon is by no means an unusual problem. Don't forget that the brake pedal goes up and down just like the accelerator, so you get either more effect or less effect, depending on how far you have pressed it. If you are slowing down too much therefore, and look like stopping too soon, well just lift your foot off the brake. The car won't speed up again but just roll on under its own momentum, so you can brake again when you are a little nearer your intended stopping place.

When you just wish to reduce speed, rather than stop, don't press the brake pedal for too long. As soon as your speed is reduced to the level you want, lift off the brake otherwise you will go more and more slowly and eventually stop altogether, which is not really the effect you wanted.

Stopping really smoothly is a delight to behold, particularly from the passenger's viewpoint. If you read the road ahead and anticipate the actions of other road users and work out your own programme in good time, you should rarely have to brake hard. When you have to stop, slow down in good time, use your brakes gently and just before you actually stop, reduce the pedal pressure so that at the actual moment of stopping you have almost no brakes on at all. If you think about it you need far less pedal pressure to stop from 5 mph than you do to stop from 30 mph. So bring your speed gently down, and when you're down to walking speed, slacken the pressure on the pedal and you'll whisper to a stop almost unnoticeably. The examiner will thoroughly approve.

Don't brake for every visible hazard. Often, lifting off the gas pedal for a few seconds is quite sufficient to cater for the situation, whereas braking would bring the speed down more than is necessary, to the point of needing a change down to a lower gear. In other words, don't over-react, it's poor judgement.

What really should be done in situations like this is something which often fails to occur to the candidate. I'm talking about the need to cover the brake with the right foot, without actually pressing or applying the brake.

There are many situations where a potential hazard exists, where the need to stop quite suddenly might arise. Children playing on the side of the road heedless of the approaching vehicle; turning at a junction round a sharp, blind corner; there are many such situations where one can see the learner driver's foot still over the gas pedal. True, they have lifted off the gas to slow down, but the foot is there, ready to accelerate away when the danger is past. The foot should of course be hovering over the brake pedal.

In these situations, if any one of the six controls is going to be wanted in a hurry, it is surely the brake pedal, and that is where the foot should be, ready for instant use should the need arise.

Not having the foot ready to brake when a hazard is ahead is a major fault with many drivers, new and experienced, and a frequent cause of test failure.

Handbrake

You are expected to use the handbrake at the right time and in the right manner. Never use the handbrake to either slow down or stop the vehicle – except in the very unlikely event of a failure of the main braking system, virtually unheard of today.

What this means is **never apply the handbrake when the vehicle is moving**. Pupils frequently do this without actually intending to do so. They have been asked to pull up, and they know that when stopped, they are going to apply the handbrake. What happens so often is that as the speed comes down, the learner driver's left hand goes down to the handbrake in anticipation, and before the car has actually stopped, the handbrake is pulled sharply on. Do this on test, and two things will result. One is a possible rear wheel skid, and the other is almost certain failure of the test.

Apply the handbrake only when the vehicle is stationary, keeping both hands on the steering wheel until then. Apply it correctly, that is to say, quietly. Press the button on top of the brake lever, pull the brake up tight, let go the button then pull the brake up through a couple of final 'clicks'.

Your instructor will demonstrate this drill early on. You should carefully avoid the habit of allowing the lever to 'click' over the ratchet throughout its length of travel. This will only wear out the ratchet mechanism, and it makes a horrible noise.

Using the handbrake at the right time really means don't overdo it. The days are long gone when a driver was supposed to apply the handbrake at every 'Give Way' sign. The fact is that at many junctions it is often unnecessary to come to a complete stop. If you do stop and **are on level ground**, a handbrake is not necessary if you are moving off again almost immediately. If you stop on an **uphill** slope however, then a handbrake is a must, otherwise you will roll backwards when trying to move off, a major fault for sure.

If you stop, say at traffic lights, in a queue of traffic, then a handbrake is advisable. Why? Well, if the vehicle coming up behind you should happen to run into your rear – and it does happen – then you will not be bounced forward into the vehicle in front of you.

A similar situation is the occasion when you are waiting in the right hand lane near the centre of the road waiting to turn to the right, and are held up by oncoming traffic. If you have a long line of approaching traffic and therefore a wait of more than a few seconds, again, apply the handbrake. A shunt from the rear could push you straight into the path of an oncoming vehicle, and the handbrake would prevent this.

When you make a normal stop, apply the handbrake before putting the gear into neutral. When you move off again, it's the other way round; into gear then handbrake off. Getting these the wrong way round is certainly not a major fault, but a fault just the same.

The final often-committed fault on handbrake is do make sure that when you let the handbrake off before moving, you let it right off. It is only too easy to let it partly off and move away. You would probably get a red warning light on the dashboard, and the examiner would certainly notice it. Maybe you have let the lever down far enough to release the brakes, but on the other hand the rear brakes could be binding on the brake drums. This is potentially dangerous, and cars have caught fire through over-heated brakes, the handbrake having been left partly on.

Use of the handbrake is like use of signals, which we'll come to later. It should be used following some conscious thought, not just through habit.

Steering

A steering fault usually lies in one of two areas. It's either due to careless or incorrect handling of the steering wheel – even though you are following a correct course – or it's down to allowing the car to be in the wrong place on the road.

Incorrect handling of the steering wheel is a very common driving fault, and to avoid it you must be comfortable in your driving position. Your instructor will go through all this with you on your very first lesson. Don't have the seat too far forward, you don't want the steering wheel in your chest. Nor do you want the straight-armed 'boy racer' position. You should aim to have your arms slightly bent when holding the wheel with your hands in the 'ten to two' or 'quarter to three' position.

Keep your thumbs on the front of the wheel, where you can see them, not curled round the back. Hold the wheel lightly, no white knuckles. You will wander all over the road if you grip too tightly. Fingers should be lightly curled round the rim of the wheel, hands kept in position just by their own weight. Now drop your wrists a little so that the first two fingers on each hand begin to point upwards. Your index fingers should now be almost pointing around the rim of the wheel, thumbs visible in front. What you must certainly avoid is gripping the wheel as if you were holding a heavy jug by its handle, or even a pint of bitter.

On straight roads with little camber you will find the car will follow a straight course almost by itself. Only take a firmer grip when actually turning. When turning, don't snatch at the wheel, pass it smoothly from hand-to-hand, pulling down with one hand and pushing up with the other. This technique is well described and illustrated on page 21 of *The Driving Manual*. They describe it as the push and pull method; what they really mean is the pull and push, since you pull down on one side before pushing up on the other.

Take care not to allow either hand to go beyond the twelve o'clock position, and then you should never find yourself with 'crossed hands'. Crossing hands means having your left hand to the right of your right hand and vice versa. Always keep each hand on its own side of the wheel. Crossing hands will earn you a steering fault, except when doing a reversing manoeuvre. When reversing you may steer in any manner you find comfortable.

Never allow both hands to be on the same side of the steering wheel. Imagine having the steering wheel bisected by a line running from 12 o'clock to 6 o'clock, like this:

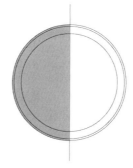

Always have one hand on the shaded side of the wheel and the other on the unshaded. Having both hands on the same side of the wheel will certainly earn you a steering fault. This correct pull and push steering comes quite naturally to some people and for others it is difficult to grasp. Two forms of practice can help a great deal. One is to get hold of the household's round coffee tray. Sit down, holding the tray like a steering wheel. Practise turning it to the left, then the right, passing it from hand-to-hand – pull and push.

I suggest you lock yourself in the loo for this practice because doing it in public usually causes the rest of the family to fall about in near hysteria, making helpful comments like 'mind the bus'!

A more advanced form of practice is to persuade Father to jack up the front end of the family car until the front wheels are just off the ground, and then you can practise steering drill without traffic or hassle. One important thing – never turn the steering wheel of a car when it is stationary, even with power steering. Doing so will ruin the front tyres very rapidly. Jack it up first to avoid excessive wear on the tread of the tyres.

Another frequent steering fault is to allow the steering wheel to straighten up by itself after a turn. The steering geometry in the attitude of the front wheels of a car is such that, after a turn, the front wheels will straighten themselves up as the car continues to go forward. A driver should, however, control this straightening up by passing the wheel from hand-to-hand during the unwinding process, not just let go of the wheel and allow it to spin back uncontrolled by itself. Called 'slipping the wheel', this is a sure recipe for test failure.

A couple of sections back, when discussing gears, we spoke of the laid back character who cruises along with the left hand resting on the gear lever, as if it were in imminent danger of popping out of its socket. This is really a steering fault; two hands on the wheel being a great deal better than one.

So far we have dealt with faults which are based on incorrect handling of the steering wheel. The other type of steering fault, you remember, involves the car being in the wrong place on the road.

Take care when turning left or right into side roads. If you turn too soon when turning right, you will most likely cut the corner and find yourself on the wrong side of the road you've just turned into, and probably face-to-face with some innocent citizen coming the other way.

Turning the wheel too late on a right turn means swinging wide and probably striking the kerb or even mounting the footpath on the left, or nearside.

Turning too soon when turning left usually puts your nearside rear wheel up over the kerb as you go round the corner, and turning too late on a left turn results in again swinging wide, thus putting you out beyond the centre of the road you are turning into, and this in turn places you in a head-on situation to approaching vehicles.

Quite a number of faults can be linked with more than one of our 22 sections or headings. An example of this is in the previous paragraph. Finding yourself in the wrong place on the road at a junction, as a result of a steering fault, actually overlaps with

Section 15 of the test, which deals with *'positioning properly at road junctions with regard to turning right or left'* (see page 114).

Whenever you find yourself in the wrong place on the road, it is always down to either bad forward planning or inaccurate steering.

Be careful not to collect a steering fault when pulling up at the kerb. Don't try to be too clever, and park with your nearside wheels a centimetre from the kerb. If you misjudge it slightly and clout or scrape the kerb, you will have collected a steering fault (and probably damaged a tyre). Sitting in the driver's seat, it is not easy to know exactly where the nearside wheels are. Do remember to use the nearside door mirror as you approach the kerb to pull up. In the mirror, if it is correctly adjusted, you should be able to see both the side of the car and the kerbstone. The examiner does not expect you to be a centimetre from the kerb, nor of course will he accept parking a metre away, 12 or 15 centimetres or so is fine, and remember, it's better to be a bit too far away from the kerb rather than actually scraping it.

This chapter, on Section 3 of the test, is really six sub-sections, all to do with controlling the vehicle confidently and smoothly, and this means being able to smoothly coordinate all the controls together. In each sub-section we have seen examples of how to mishandle the car, and these are all potential faults to avoid. For this reason your instructor will concentrate in the early stages on how the car works and how to control it. It is really important to become proficient in these basic skills before getting into the finer points of coping with town traffic. If you can operate the car smoothly and efficiently before getting too involved in more advanced driving and traffic theory, it will make you much more confident.

SECTION 4 OF THE TEST

Move away safely under control

Move away safely

This is really simple, yet it is surprising how many tests are blown under this heading. To move off safely you must only move off when it is safe to do so. Now that's not complicated is it? It does mean a good effective **look in all directions** before you move. Only move away when you can do so without causing any danger or inconvenience to any other road user, and that includes pedestrians and cyclists.

If I had to specify in only one word the most essential quality of a good driver, that word would have to be **observation**. It applies in so many driving contexts and it certainly applies when moving off. You **look**. You look ahead for approaching traffic, you take in the sides, the footpaths for pedestrians about to cross, and you look to the rear for traffic approaching from behind.

For this rear observation, the rearview mirror is not enough, neither is the side door mirror. A passing cyclist who is almost level with you as you are about to set off, is in a blind spot which is not covered by either of these mirrors. For this reason we **always** check over the right shoulder before moving.

This right shoulder check comes after we've done everything else. After starting the engine, after fastening seat belts, after getting into gear, after checking the internal mirror, finally look over the right shoulder. It is no good looking behind for the cyclist and then doing all those other things, and then starting to move. Believe me, that is when the phantom cyclist appears from nowhere. A stretch of road which was empty when you looked can become very much occupied a matter of five or six seconds later.

Do you need to check over your left shoulder? If you are moving away from a position which is more than a metre or so from the kerb, the answer is definitely yes. You might have done an emergency stop for a carelessly crossing pedestrian, in which case you won't have pulled up by the kerb. There could well be a two metre gap on your left, and a gap like that is a great challenge to a small boy on a bicycle. Similarly, if you are moving away at traffic lights, look over your left shoulder first, particularly if you are about to turn left. That is where the cyclists will be lurking.

If you are stuck behind a large parked vehicle, having given way to oncoming traffic, you are going to have to move off at an angle in order to pass it. This situation calls for careful checks to the rear, in case another driver is planning to pass both you and the stationary vehicle in one go. Careful observation for oncoming traffic is also needed. As the illustration shows, don't stop right up close behind the obstruction, or too near to the kerb, otherwise you will have no line of sight to the front to help you establish when it is safe to move on.

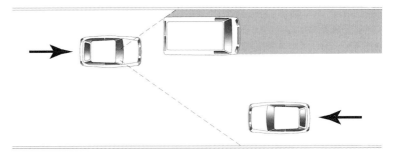

Whatever position you are moving away from, look everywhere, including all three mirrors and the blind spots. Never move away until you can do so without any inconvenience to others. Whenever you move off the examiner will be watching critically.

Move away under control

Moving away under control was really covered previously under section 3 of the test, where we dealt with using all six major car controls. If you are clumsy with these controls, either separately or in conjunction with each other, you will get a clumsy, rough start. You could stall the engine, use the wrong gear, fail to coordinate the handbrake and clutch, let the clutch up too sharply, use too little or too much accelerator, scrape your wheels along the kerb, and so on. The scope for a real booboo is rarely greater than when moving away.

The interesting thing is that if you commit any of these errors, the examiner won't mark them under *'make proper use of clutch, accelerator, gears, handbrake'* or whatever. It would be marked under the widespread umbrella of section 4 – *'move away under control'.*

He won't exactly balance a coin on top of the dashboard when you move away, but he will want to see a good display of smooth control and coordination of handbrake, clutch and accelerator.

One way to move away (and stop) smoothly is to imagine you have your favourite drink perched on top of the dashboard; a pint of Guinness, gin and tonic, Bacardi and Coke or a mug of Horlicks, whatever - but it must be full to the brim. Now make sure you move off, and stop, without spilling a drop. I find this an effective way to get pupils to carry out these basic tasks really smoothly, and if you can do this on test it all helps to give the impression that you are in full control of the car. (See page 42 'footbrake' on smooth braking.)

Be prepared for the examiner to ask you to pull up for no apparent reason, perhaps several times, and maybe behind a parked vehicle. He's watching your skill and judgement at both pulling up and moving off again.

SECTION 5 OF THE TEST

Emergency stop

The driving examiner must be satisfied that you can stop the vehicle in an emergency, '*promptly*' and '*under control*'.

'*Promptly*' is self-explanatory. You must react quickly and firmly. If an elderly lady falls in the road, 20 metres ahead of you and you stop in 17 metres, you all live happily ever after. If you take 23 metres in which to stop, you have spoilt her afternoon, to put it mildly.

There is a great deal more to stopping quickly and safely than just slamming on the brakes as hard as you can. It is not the purpose of this book to teach you how to do everything, our main purpose is to tell you what not to do. Your instructor will go through the emergency stop drill with you, and you will practise it until you are confident.

DON'T stall the engine when you stop; and DON'T lock the wheels and skid.

'*Under control*' is the part where candidates usually go wrong. Under control really boils down to two 'don'ts': DON'T stall the engine when you stop; and DON'T lock the wheels and skid.

To avoid stalling the engine we must, at some time during all the excitement, press the clutch down before we stop.

To avoid locking the wheels and inducing a skid needs a little thought. First of all, stopping quickly needs pretty firm braking but if we brake too hard, the wheels stop revolving and the momentum of the car causes the tyres to lose their grip on the road surface. So the wheels aren't going round but the car is still moving, and that is a skid. When the car is skidding, we have lost control, we cannot steer.

Let's look at what happens when you brake hard. Well, you probably already know; everything gets thrown forwards, doesn't it? The maps fly off the back shelf, the dog goes on the floor and Aunty lurches forward in her seat belt. The main thing, however, is that about 75 per cent of the weight of the car also gets thrown forward, over onto the front wheels in fact. Now this is good, because all that weight over the front end pushes the front wheels really hard down onto the road, the area of front tyre actually in contact with the road is increased and the front tyres have now got a really good grip. Much more grip than when you are riding along straight and level, not accelerating, not braking.

This is the key to a rapid, safe stop. Stab the brake pedal firmly, not hard enough to lock the wheels and skid, but hard enough to fetch the maps off the shelf, and throw all that weight forward, over the front end. Then, and only then, do you complete the braking action. Squeeze the brakes – not another stab – a steady squeeze, tighter and tighter. The speed is coming down very rapidly now, and the lower the speed the less likelihood of locking the wheels and skidding. When you do stop it is with a pretty hard jerk, and you have the brake pedal pressed down about as hard as you can. But it didn't get down there all at once. If you had braked that hard right at the start, you would certainly have locked the wheels and skidded out of control.

So it is a progressive braking process. The sharp stab, followed by the steady squeeze, then de-clutch as the speed comes down. When the examiner gives you the signal to stop, **don't** hit the clutch first, he won't accept it. Brake first, then clutch. The rapid deceleration continues to push the nose of the car down and those front tyres will stop you firmly. Incidentally it's not the brakes that stop a car. The brakes only stop the wheels going round; it's the tyres which stop you. They are the most important bits of gear on the car, they are your contact with Mother Earth.

Having stopped, don't sit there, heart pounding, clammy hands gripping the wheel, waiting for the examiner to pat you on the back. He won't say a word until you have finished off the job. That means handbrake and neutral then take your feet off the pedals. Only then will he say 'thank you, drive on when you are ready, and I shall not ask you to do that exercise again.'

Then what? You move off safely, checking the mirrors and looking over **both** shoulders. Why? Well you haven't stopped close to the kerb this time, and there could be a bicycle in the process of passing you on your left. You'll be expected to check both sides.

Two 'don'ts' on the emergency stop. When the examiner calls 'stop' don't waste time on the mirror. He will have checked to the rear already. You just get on with the stopping. The second 'don't' is don't attempt to steer or alter course. Harsh braking and steering don't mix. Together, they result in a side-skid.

When you've passed your test, don't forget all this. Go over it in your mind and occasionally practise it. You could go for a couple of years or more before you have to stop in haste, but when the child does run out in front of you, there's no time to rehearse. No mirror, just stab and squeeze. Don't panic and slam the brakes on regardless, you'll skid and lose control. Getting it right could save a life one day; it could be yours.

SECTION 6 OF THE TEST

Reversing into a side road

Drivers can be divided into many groups and two of these groups, particularly among learners, are those who can drive backwards with the same level of instinctive directional judgement which they have when going forward, and those who can't.

We probably learned to steer at the age of 18 months or so when our parents pushed us along in our first pedal car. If only these negligent parents had pushed us backwards occasionally, what a lot of heartache and aggro it would have saved in later years.

Once again, we're not going in detail into how to steer backwards round a corner. Your instructor will give you guidance on this, and plenty of practice. We are going to look at the common mistakes which often cause test failure.

You may think you are hopeless at reversing, and once you've passed the test you will never reverse again. But of course you won't pass the test until you can do it, and you never know when the occasion may arise when you've really got to reverse.

To illustrate this, in our local town we have a very narrow one-way street. Leading onto this road is the exit from a shoppers' car park. On leaving the car park you are faced with this sign: TURN RIGHT ONLY, which is clear enough. No problem.

One fine morning I had directed my pupil to turn into this narrow one-way street, and half-way along we met a small car piloted by an elderly lady, going the wrong way. She had obviously come out of the car park and turned left instead of right. We both stopped, nose-to-nose. I got out and walked to her car. She wound down the window and raised impatient, autocratic eyebrows.

'Yes?' she enquired.

A lady to her very fingertips, her immaculately dressed blue rinsed hair was surmounted by a shapeless, gold coloured velvet hat. It sat atop her regal head like a distorted omelette. With the courtesy for which we driving instructors are justly famous I said 'Madam, I fear you are going down a one-way street the wrong way'. The omelette quivered.

'Nonsense young man' she declared firmly.

I liked that bit, having personally been driving for a little over 45 years. With great respect I pointed out that she had turned the wrong way on leaving the car park, and that there was a prominent arrow to the right displayed at the exit.

'Oh dear, what should I do?' she enquired anxiously.

'Well' I said 'You simply reverse a few yards back into the car park, and set off again to the right.'

She stared at me, aghast, as if having learned that the butler was systematically poisoning the port.

'Reverse?' she quavered. 'You mean go backwards?'

I gave her an encouraging nod.

'Oh no young man' she declared firmly, 'Oh indeed no, I never go backwards'.

This was delivered with the firm conviction of one who had not driven backwards since before the war, and was not about to start now.

We eventually extricated her from the car, reversed it into the car park and got her reinstalled. The lady resumed her stately way, expressing gratitude to me and condemnation of the local authority for erecting impertinent and ridiculous traffic signs which prevented her negotiating public roads in her chosen direction.

So, you must be able to drive backwards, often in a tight, restricted situation. You never know when there might be no alternative. If you don't have reversing as a God-given talent take heart. You can practise at home once your instructor has shown you what is required, and the principles involved.

On the test you must reverse round a corner '*under control*'. This takes us back to basic car handling techniques, particularly clutch control and steering. Don't stall the engine, don't try to move with the handbrake still on, don't try to move backwards in a 'forward' gear and so on. All basic stuff really. The principal task among these handling skills is, of course, to steer a correct course.' which needs practice, practice and more practice.

Please note that since 1990, anyone driving on a provisional licence must be accompanied by someone who holds a full licence to drive the vehicle the learner is driving. Further, the person supervising must have held the appropriate licence for 3 years and be at least 21 years old. Make sure that the person accompanying you for practice meets these requirements.

If you turn the steering wheel **too soon**, i.e. before the back of the car is level with the point where the kerbstone actually starts to curve round, you will hit the kerbstone. Similarly if you turn the steering wheel too much you turn in an arc which is smaller than the curve of the corner, again you will touch the kerb. Touching the kerb with either front or rear wheel is a major control fault, and means failure. Make sure that when you set off to reverse round the corner, your nearside (left) wheels are at least 0.5 metre away from the kerb. Give yourself a bit of elbow room.

Having warned you not to get too close to the kerb and touch it, don't get too far away from it either. The opposite of the previous paragraph is true. If you turn your steering wheel either **too late** or **not far enough**, you will swing wide round the corner and finish up with part of your car beyond the centre of the road into which you are reversing. Figure 1 below, makes this clear.

In my experience the most frequent control fault in this manoeuvre is keeping on turning too far round the corner. You then strike the kerb with the nearside rear wheel, at a point where the **kerbstone** has straightened up, but **you** have not. Figure 2 below, makes this clear.

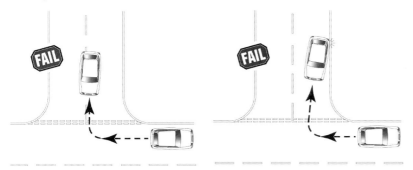

Figure 1   Figure 2

There is a simple remedy for this which you can use during practice while you are learning to straighten up at the correct moment. Keep your speed down as you come round the corner, by slipping the clutch. At no point in these reversing manoeuvres do you need your clutch fully connected – you would travel too fast. So, slowly round the corner and when the car reaches the point where it is parallel to the kerb **once the kerb has straightened up**, then stop the car, briefly. A quick glance in the nearside door mirror will confirm the position, although you should also be able to spot this point by looking through the rear window.

Having stopped you will see that you have curved round as far as you need to (usually through 90 degrees). You have not gone round too far (as in Figure 2) but if you did let the car travel any further, you would have your tail end pointing at the kerb. Why? Because the front wheels of the car are still turned at an angle to steer you round the corner.

It follows then, that we need to straighten the steering wheel, quickly, before we curve round any more. Many pupils have a mental blank at this point. Which way do we turn the steering wheel to centre the front wheels? It's not as daft as it sounds, many people have this problem when going backwards. Just have faith in the fact that it's the same as going forwards. If you have turned the steering wheel to the left to go round the corner (which you have), you must turn it to the right to get things back to normal. That's what happens going round a corner forwards, the same drill applies when in reverse.

Once you have decided that you are going to turn the wheel to the right to straighten up, start to move back slowly and at the same time turn the steering wheel to the right as quickly as possible, so that before you have travelled more than a quarter metre, the front wheels of the car are pointing exactly to the front, and you are travelling in an absolute straight line. When turning the steering wheel to the **right** to straighten up, be careful not to turn it too far. If you do you will be starting to turn the front wheels to the **right**, which will cause the back of the car to curve out towards the centre of the road.

Two things will help you gain confidence and accuracy in reversing. Plenty of practice is more than half the battle, and the other thing is to keep the speed right down as you practise. In due course you will become more proficient and able to do the job a little more briskly.

Incidentally, the examiner may ask you to reverse into a side road to the right. This is not often done, and usually applies to people who turn up for the test in a van with no side windows other than driver's and passenger's. Your instructor should see that you get practice at reversing to both right and left. Reversing to the right is much simpler, it's easier to see where you are going.

Touching the kerb or in any other way steering a wrong course, or mishandling the car, these are all 'control faults'. The other area in which a fault can occur is 'with proper observation'. Faults here are usually due to another road user turning up, be it vehicle, cyclist or pedestrian. The test candidate either fails to see the other road user, or fails to take the correct action. When you are concentrating on the dreaded manoeuvre, inching your way round the corner, tongue slightly protruding, legs shaking, eyes cast Heavenward in silent prayer; it is easy to overlook some other road user who arrives on the scene without you noticing, but you must act correctly.

You must therefore keep a good look all around you when reversing, and the examiner will watch you closely to see if you are carrying out this essential observation. As a pedestrian, I have been knocked down by a car which was being driven backwards while the driver was looking forwards, so I speak with feeling.

If, as you reverse up to the corner, any vehicle or cyclist approaches you either from behind or in front, you must stop until it has passed. Secondly, having started to reverse into the side road, if a vehicle comes up behind you, wishing to emerge from the road you are entering, stop and see if he elects to go past you. If he doesn't and comes to a stop behind you, then you must go forward again round the corner to your starting position, and when he has gone you will have to start your manoeuvre again. Finally, keep a good look out for pedestrians, they have a habit of stepping out to cross the road behind you. You must know they are there, and you must stop for them.

The guideline here is simple, it is the same for all other motoring situations. You must not endanger or inconvenience any other road user, but if you don't keep 'proper observation', you won't know they are there.

At one time the examiner's marking sheet called for 'due regard for other road users' on these reversing manoeuvres, instead of 'proper observation'. Proper observation is even more demanding, so whether or not you have the area to yourself you must be seen to be looking about you throughout the entire manoeuvre, not just concentrating on the left hand kerb or your door mirror.

I cannot emphasise strongly enough this need for all-round observation when manoeuvring. Reversing certainly calls for much concentration if you are to do it accurately, but it is NOT sufficient just to get the steering right. If you are not seen to be taking adequate observation all around you, you will be penalised. It is an all too common failure point, and very disappointing to do a copy book piece of reversing only to find you have been major-faulted for lack of observation.

SECTION 7 OF THE TEST

Turning in the road

This section of the test requires you to turn in the road *'under control'* and *'with proper observation'*. The examiner is looking for the same set of standards for the turn in the road as for the reverse round the corner. The reasons for failure therefore, are almost identical.

The examiner, having found a road suitable for the exercise, will ask you to pull up somewhere convenient on the left-hand side. This means convenient, safe, sensible and legal. The choice of actual stopping place is up to you. Notice that the examiner then asks you to turn the car round using the forward and reverse gears, he does not ask you to do a 'three point turn'. If the road is rather narrow, or your car has a poor steering lock, i.e. needs a large turning circle, it may be that you will need more than three moves in which to turn round. You may need to put in two more moves, thus doing a five point turn.

Now this is where a learner is often misled. Many books on learning to drive – including *The Driving Test* – tend to illustrate a turn in the road as in Figure 1, like this:

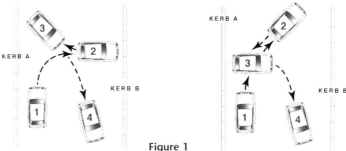

KERB A

KERB A

KERB B

KERB B

Figure 1

Figure 2

At the end of the first move, the car is shown as having turned through at least 90 degrees and to be square-on to the right-hand kerb (kerb B). So, at the end of the second move (the reverse leg), the car is almost facing in the opposite direction, ready to be driven away with only a little right-hand steering needed. In fact, this only happens in a generously wide road.

What is more likely to happen on the test is that you will be asked to turn round in a rather narrower road, one that will test your steering abilities to a greater degree. In this case the situation in Figure 2 will be more applicable. The car does not achieve an angle of 90 degrees to kerb B until the end of the second leg (position 3), and so some very brisk steering will be called for in order to avoid scraping kerb B as you drive away. Remember, it's not easy, sitting in the right hand seat, to judge where the nearside wheels are. If you think there is ANY chance of scraping kerb B with your front nearside wheel, do two more legs as follows.

When you are close to kerb B on your 3rd leg, steer briskly to the left, stop, and reverse to the middle of the road again. Turn the wheels once more to the right, stop, and drive away. So you have done a five point turn instead of a three, under complete control.

In a narrow road, the examiner will expect you to do this rather than risk scraping kerb B as you exit the turn.

Apart from a narrow road, you could meet with one extra problem.

So far we have assumed that we are turning round on a fairly flat road, one with little camber, like this:

Consider the task of turning round on a road with a steep camber, usually an older road, like this:

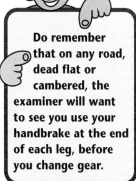

The added hazard here is that at the end of each leg, when you stop and change either into or out of reverse gear, you have quite a steep hill start to cope with. A control problem again.

You are going to have to coordinate your clutch, handbrake and accelerator carefully otherwise you will roll down the short stretch of incline, and zonk the kerb. Failure again due to poor control.

'Kerbing' means failure since you don't have the vehicle under full control. Don't risk touching the kerb.

Do remember that on any road, dead flat or cambered, the examiner will want to see you use your handbrake at the end of each leg, before you change gear.

63

So much for control. Now what about *'proper observation'*? Well, as with reversing round a corner, don't get so wrapped up in your manoeuvre that you forget the observation. If any other road user turns up, you MUST see them coming – double decker bus or a little lad on a bike.

Before you set off for the other side of the road **look** all round. Up and down the road, mirrors, right shoulder check. If another road user is approaching, stay where you are until they have passed. Once you have set off across the road however, if someone comes into view along your road, don't stop and go back. Carry on and finish off that leg. Wait (with either your nose or your tail in the gutter) and see what they do. They will either drive past the end of your car and disappear, or they will stop a little way away and wait for you to finish your task. Don't wave them on, let them decide what they want to do. Once you are satisfied that they really do intend to wait for you to finish, just get on with the job, but look the other way first. Someone may have turned up from the opposite direction while you had paused to see what the first vehicle was doing.

Once you are satisfied that other vehicles are stationary and intend to remain so, finish your manoeuvre without delay or hesitation, so as not to inconvenience the other drivers. Don't rush it however. Don't let them put you under pressure, because you are sure to miss bits out and mess it up. It was, after all, their decision to wait for you to finish, rather than driving past the end of your car, which they could have done if they had been in a tearing hurry.

The same principles apply to all three of these reversing exercises.

Keep the speed down and the car under control. *Above all keep constant all round observation.*

SECTION 8 OF THE TEST

Reverse (or parallel) park

Early in 1993 the long overdue requirement to reverse park the vehicle was added to the test. You are learning to park your car in a space between two other vehicles, but on a test it is difficult to find two cars with a convenient space between them when wanted, so the test requires reverse parking behind a stationary vehicle, usually with a long empty space behind it. The examiner will ask you, however, to confine your manoeuvre so that you finish parked within two car lengths of the vehicle concerned.

There is a diagram of the manoeuvre in *The Driving Test*, and with acknowledgement to the *Daily Telegraph*, I reproduce a similar diagram of a vehicle (car A) which has come forward from the left of the diagram and stopped beside car 2. There should be a gap between the two cars of just under 1 metre, and the door mirror of car A should be roughly level with the front end of car 2. (Remember, in the test, car 1 will not actually be there).

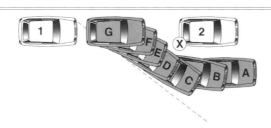

The trouble with both diagrams is that, although they show the path you follow when reversing in behind a parked car, neither one shows the position of the front (or steering) wheels during the manoeuvre.

I don't intend to give you chapter and verse on how to steer as you reverse into a parking space, your instructor will do that and he will give you plenty of essential practice. We will concentrate on what you must not do.

Now that reverse parking has been with us for a few years, most pupils seem to think it is not too difficult. Certainly it does not seem to be held in such dread as reversing round a corner, and it is without doubt the most useful of the three manoeuvres and the one you will use most often once you have passed.

You can of course get it wrong, as with any manoeuvre, and if you are going to fail on this one, there are four common faults to choose from. If you start from too far in front of the parked car alongside you, and you put on left lock too soon (i.e. towards the kerb) you could clout him with the back of your car as you curve round towards the kerb. Secondly, if you miss him with your rear end, you could then turn on to right lock too soon and catch him with your front end.

Fortunately candidates don't commit either of these errors very often, but they do go for error number three – starting the manoeuvre with too wide a gap between themselves and the stationary vehicle. (i.e. too far out towards the centre of the road). They do the necessary bit of left and right steering, but finish up a couple of metres away from the kerb. It is easily done, but also easy to cure – by making sure that you start in the right position.

The fourth fault is also easy to commit. It involves putting on too much left lock at the start of the job, and this results in the car assuming much too great an angle to the kerb, almost right angles sometimes. It is then not possible to put on enough right lock to bring the car round parallel to the kerb, and so the rear nearside wheel either strikes or actually mounts the kerb.

If you read this before being shown the manoeuvre, all the talk about steering first left then right will only confuse you. Wait until you have had a couple of tries at it, then the description of the possible mistakes will actually mean something.

This manoeuvre is mainly about steering but all other car control functions are equally important; as in the other two manoeuvres – coordinate clutch and accelerator, don't stall, keep the speed down. The mixture as before, in fact. Similarly with *'proper observation'*, take a good look in both directions before moving out to start the manoeuvre. Wait until there is no traffic approaching from front or rear before starting. Stop if any vehicle approaches you after you have started. If they cannot get by whilst you are alongside the vehicle you propose to park behind, then finish off the task and get out of their way in the process. Don't delay them unnecessarily, but don't be pressured and rush it – you'll probably spoil it.

That should be the end of this reversing manoeuvre section, but you might find it helpful to spend a little more time on this parking business. Many drivers are not really comfortable when reversing, and to some, parking seems to be a nightmare. For a start, why do we have to reverse into a parking space, why not drive in forwards? Either the car will fit into the space or it won't. It can't make any difference, forwards or backwards. Logical, you might think, but unfortunately, not true.

It is quite true that you can drive forwards into a parking space if it's long enough, but nowadays spaces are pretty small, assuming you can find one at all. The trouble is that if you drive into a limited space forwards, you will leave your rear end sticking out. This is because the back wheels don't steer, or swivel like the front ones, so the result looks like this:–

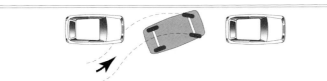

However by reversing in and positioning the back wheels near the kerb, and then turning the steering wheel to the right, the front of the car will swing to the **left** towards the kerb. You then finish close to and parallel to the kerb, like this:–

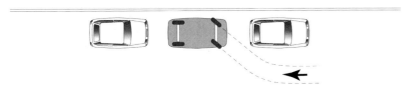

We just said 'turn the steering wheel to the **right** and the front of the car will swing to the **left**' (whilst reversing). Does that statement bother you? It probably does take some swallowing. It seems clear to a new driver that if you're going forwards and turn the wheel to the right, the front of the car will also swing to the right.

That part is easy to accept. But when going in reverse, if you turn the steering wheel to the right, the front of the car swings to the left, although the back still goes to the right and the rest of the car seems to follow! That bit seems illogical, confusing and hard to swallow.

Don't lose any sleep thinking about it. A short demonstration by your instructor should soon make it clear. It is this little titbit of driving know-how which forms the basis of all reversing manoeuvres. It is failure to come to terms with the question of which way to steer when reversing which causes test candidates to hit the kerb having reversed round a corner.

Time and time again candidates turn the steering wheel the wrong way when straightening up, and that's why this point is so important. Don't just hope it will go away if you don't think about it. Have it demonstrated to you, learn, practise and understand it. The real key to getting on top of steering in reverse is practice, and more practice.

Sections 6, 7 and 8 of the test have dealt with your reversing manoeuvres, but finally some advice that refers to them all.

In the late summer of 1996 the Driving Standards Agency unveiled two important requirements which apply to all the reversing exercises. Believe me, your examiner will really be on the lookout for them.

The first point concerns 'dry steering'. What on earth is dry steering? You may well ask. Essentially, 'dry steering' is turning the steering wheel when the car is stationary. It is hard work – unless your car is blessed with power assisted steering – and it is ruinous to the front tyres.

If you think about it, if the wheels are not rotating and you manage to turn the steering wheel with much heaving and straining and bulging biceps, the small area of tyre at the bottom of the wheel, i.e. in contact with the road, takes an awful lot of stick. You are in fact doing your best to scrub all the tread off it.

Cars with power steering usually get through a set of front tyres more quickly than those without. The reason is that dry steering can be done with little noticeable effort. It is a bad habit and bad driving.

During your reversing exercises therefore, even if you are fast running out of road space, have your car actually moving, however slowly, while you turn the steering wheel. You will certainly be faulted for 'dry steering' if you don't.

The second recent requirement is to complete your reversing manoeuvres 'within a reasonable time'. This is so as to avoid undue delay to other vehicles. Reasonable enough.

Don't rush – you'll forget something vital, but don't take all day.

SECTION 9 OF THE TEST

Use of mirror and rear observation

To satisfy the examiner in this section of the test the driver of a vehicle must make effective rear observation at appropriate times, and this is usually – though not always – covered by the other requirement in the same section – to make effective use of mirrors. The separate mention of rear observation is aimed principally at motorcyclists who are not usually as well equipped with mirrors as are car drivers.

A very common cause of both test failure and traffic accidents is failure to use mirrors. I well remember a friend of ours who proudly showed us her new drophead, which had a door mirror on the offside only. I suggested that the only thing the car needed to make it absolutely 100 per cent perfect was a nearside door mirror.

'Good grief, John' was the instant reply 'I have enough trouble seeing what's going on in front without bothering with mirrors'.

I couldn't really answer that without seeming really pompous, but I'm afraid she's not alone by any means.

This section really needs no explanation, it means what it says, and if you don't make intelligent and effective use of mirrors, you will fail. We will go in for some explanation, however, because it is no good your instructor telling you 'always check your mirror before signalling or before you slow down etc. etc.' An intelligent pupil is going to ask why.

'Why?' is a very good question, one you should ask your instructor whenever you can't see a good reason for doing what he has told you. A procedure learnt parrot fashion is useless, and will soon be discarded once you are on your own.

A good instructor will always make sure the pupil understands the reason behind any instruction. And of course there always is a reason, usually a safety-related reason.

So, let us look at why we use the mirrors so much. Let's just go back to page 39, where we discussed making proper use of gears. We talked about the drill for dealing with or approaching hazards. We had earlier decided that we need to be in the right place on the road at the right time, at the right speed for the task and in the right gear for the speed. How did we achieve this? By running through a little set drill for approaching hazards. **Must Surely Prevent Some Grief. Mirror**, **Signal**, **Position**, **Speed** and **Gear**. Remember? See how this ties in with the heading to this mirror section. **M S P S G** means that mirror comes before (a) signal (b) position change (c) reducing speed. Now why do we check mirror on these three occasions? Let's look at a few examples.

Mirror before signalling

Suppose we decide to take the next road on the right. Don't give a right signal as soon as you have decided to turn. Not yet, mirror first. Why? Well let's assume you're doing 40 mph. Unknown to you, another car is catching you up, doing 55 mph. He is travelling faster than you and so decides to overtake you. He checks to his rear and to the front: nothing coming. He signals right (for your benefit), moves out to the right and accelerates.

Now, just as he approaches the rear of your car, you put on your right indicator. What effect does this have on the overtaking driver? Panic, probably. You might be giving plenty of warning of a turn you propose to make 100 metres further on, but for all he knows you might be about to dive into the next field. (When discussing section 10 of the test we shall talk about giving signals in good time). At any rate he is sure now of one thing; your next move is likely to be to move out to your right, and here he is doing 55 mph plus and he's practically alongside you. What is worse, **you don't even know he's there**.

So, for any hazard, before signalling or altering position, mirror first. Incidentally the majority of road accidents are in urban areas, and usually when someone is turning right. The **M S P S G** routine would prevent most of these accidents.

If you are about to be overtaken **do not** signal right, and if you don't use your mirrors you won't know whether you are about to be overtaken or not.

Taking this same scenario, with you contemplating a turn and the gent coming up behind you, if you were making a left turn and had signalled without looking, the situation would not be so serious. Normally when you signal left, the driver behind knows that you are going to do one of two things, either make a left turn or pull up by the kerb. Either way you are going to slow down first and since he won't want to slow down himself, he will probably overtake you as soon as you signal.

Make no mistake though, if you give a signal without a mirror check, be it left or right, and you have a following vehicle, this is a major fault and spells failure.

Even when making a left turn a rearward check is essential. Often a motor cycle or moped rider, even a speedy cyclist, will tuck himself in just behind you, near your nearside rear corner. Bikers tucked in like this are often in a blind spot as far as your internal mirror goes, so use the door mirror as well.

Mirror before changing direction

If we take our earlier example of signalling right without checking the mirror, remember we had a car about to overtake us. We switched on a right hand indicator and gave him a nasty fright. Had we taken our intended manoeuvre a stage further and actually turned right, we should have involved both vehicles in a serious accident.

The same applies when turning left. Remember the two-wheeler tucked in just behind and to the left of us? What happens to him if we do a sudden left turn?

You simply **must know what is behind or alongside you before you change direction**, not just for a 90 degree turn into a side road but even a slight alteration, as when changing lanes.

When approaching a large junction with traffic lights, the road may well be marked out into two or more lanes, with arrows marking the road surface to ensure you take the correct lane, depending on your ultimate destination.

Again, if you need to move out to pass a parked car, check the mirror first

If you need to change lanes you must check your mirrors before doing so because traffic may be coming up behind you from either side. An unsignalled or wrongly timed lane change can cause an accident, and in the case of a two-wheeler, a fatal one.

Mirror before changing speed

Check before accelerating, you could be in the process of being overtaken. You should never speed up when being overtaken (common sense and good manners again).

It is in slowing down or stopping with no rearward check that so many drivers are at fault. This is absolutely vital because perhaps the commonest single driving fault today is driving too close to the vehicle in front. (Check your stopping distances in *The Highway Code*; full details in section 105, feet, metres and most useful, actual car lengths.)

Before slowing down then, say to turn into a side road, check your mirror to see if you are being closely followed by some comedian who is absolutely confident that he can stop in five metres at 30 mph. If you are, then you need to slow down more gradually than usual, to prevent him running into your rear. Braking more gently means braking earlier, hence the **mirror check in good time**. Your stop lights come on when you brake, and these should warn him that you are slowing down, and he should do the same. However, if he's brainless enough to follow you at that speed and at that distance, your brake lights will probably not penetrate his thinking process. You brake gently then, in order to protect both yourself and him from the consequences of his own stupidity. It's called 'driving on the brakes of the car behind', and the first thing in the whole sequence is **mirror**.

Having done your initial mirror check and before starting to slow down you would, of course, have given your left signal. This should alert the joker behind to the fact that your next move is probably going to be a reduction in speed, but don't count on it. The sad fact is that you share the Queen's Highway with a lot of total idiots. Observation and anticipation are the key to safe driving but, alas, many of your fellow travellers indulge in very little of either. You must, therefore, think for both yourself and others, and be absolutely committed to the observation process.

Don't just try to remember all the occasions when you should check your mirrors. From a very early stage in your driving career you should condition yourself.

Never to do anything with either your hands or feet without checking your mirror first.

A good driver does this automatically, and taking any sort of action without a mirror check should make you feel naked, ashamed of yourself and generally unclean. This state of mind takes time to acquire but stick at it. Once you have it you will never be caught out.

A final word; the test calls for mirror before signalling, changing direction or changing speed. They've missed one out though. There is one more occasion when a mirror is a must. Can you think what this is? No? Well it's **before opening a car door**, on either side.

Cyclists have been killed running into the edge of a car door. Doors have been wrenched off by passing vehicles and some horrific injuries inflicted. On the nearside, pedestrians are also at risk. **LOOK FIRST.**

As they say in Coronation Street, 'think on'. The mirror is not just for checking the hairdo.

We'll end this chapter with an actual example of failure on mirrors, under rather unusual circumstances. Don't let this happen to you.

My pupil, Andrew, took his test on a rather murky day. We had had a good pre-test lesson and he looked confident and capable. I watched him out to the car followed by the examiner. He read his allotted number plate and they climbed aboard. During the examiner's short briefing it started to rain, quite heavily, I watched, relieved, as Andrew switched on windscreen wipers and dipped headlights.

Half an hour later he was back – failed. I joined him in the car and with a snort of disgust and one rude word he tossed me his copy of the marking sheet. One glance was enough. The examiner had major faulted all three mirror sections, before signalling, before changing direction and before slowing down or stopping.

'For goodness sake Andrew, how did this happen?' And the sad tale unfolded. It seems that during the heavy rain, the side and rear windows all steamed up. The situation had been made worse by quite a long wait, stationary, in a traffic hold up. The windscreen had remained clear since we had, as usual, set the ventilation system to blow warm air through the windscreen demisters before the start of the test. After the other windows had completely steamed up the examiner had asked Andrew to pull up at a convenient place by the kerb.

'Now Mr Dawson' he had said, 'I cannot see anything through the rear window and neither can you. Will you please do something about it?'

Andrew had then fished the duster out of the door pocket, climbed in the back and made a rather smeary mess of the rear window. He had indeed been failed for not using his mirrors, for the simple reason that he couldn't, and the fault was his alone.

I tried to look sympathetic. 'Why didn't you open the windows an inch or so when you began to steam up, and switch on the rear window demister – you've done it before?'

'It never occurred to me' he said, doing a fair imitation of two short planks. I advised Andrew that under the Road Traffic Act of 1968 he was a great dozy steaming pillock, with which he graciously agreed.

We drove home in the traditional post-failure atmosphere of gloom and depression, Andrew lamenting his stupidity. Of course, he passed six weeks later, and is probably a better driver for having had two stabs at it. With hindsight it is easy to scoff at other people's apparently obvious and stupid mistakes. It is surprising, though, how the obvious can elude us when under pressure.

Andrew failed for not using his mirror. He couldn't use it because the back window was steamed up – a situation he had failed to correct. It might be worth noting that had this happened after July 1st 1996, the fault would have been marked under the new section 22, '*Use of ancillary controls*'. Failure to use the heated rear window facility would have been the major fault.

Either way, as we said earlier, don't let it happen to you.

SECTION 10 OF THE TEST

Signalling

What exactly is a signal? It is a means of communicating to other road users either your presence or your intentions. The earliest of these signals required a motorist to have a man walking in front with a red flag, to indicate presence! Although that was a bit before my time I do remember that my earliest copy of *The Highway Code* actually had diagrams of coachmen's whip signals. I wish I had kept it, it would be a collector's item now.

How many signals can you think of, which relate to driving a vehicle? Well there are eight, and they are as follows:

Horn
Indicators
Hand signals (Illustrated in *The Highway Code*)
Flashed headlights
Hazard warning lights
High intensity rear fog lights (under certain circumstances)
Brake Lights
Reversing lights

In addition to these authorised means of communication, there are other optional signals which normally require an open window plus one or more fingers, but these do not indicate either presence or intention – merely some form of displeasure – and are a matter for personal preference. However they are neither required nor recommended on test! They are not really desirable at any time, bearing in mind one of our definitions of good driving, i.e. 'good manners and common sense'.

Let's look at our eight signals in turn.

Horn

For some reason, many learner drivers seem to think it is an offence to sound a horn. Others don't even know where to find it. A horn toot gives an audible warning of your approach when you cannot be seen. Examples are when approaching a narrow hump-backed bridge or a sharp bend at a blind corner. It is also a quick way of alerting another road user who is about to put himself in danger. Examples: a cyclist in front of you, about to do a right turn without the 'life saver' look behind. A child about to dash into the road. 3.45 pm, school is out, two lads having a friendly but frenzied tussle on the footpath. One of them is bound to be shoved into the road. Let them know of the approaching danger. In circumstances like these a quick beep on the horn can save many a grievous injury.

A quick thought about lunch time or afternoon tests. When schools are coming out a test candidate's biggest hazard is usually kids on bikes, on foot, on skateboards, whatever. Adding to the confusion, mums in cars collecting their brood. They tend not so much to park their cars as abandon them, and of course there are the lollipop ladies who step out in front of unwary motorists, brandishing their magic wands.

Whenever there are kiddies about, do have the horn finger and the brake foot ready for action. Remember – observation, anticipation.

When sounding the horn, don't give a series of toots like a morse code message. One toot of about a second is enough. Used like this the horn is an effective warning. Remember it is a warning, not a rebuke. Long loud blasts are offensive. The horn should not be used in a 'get out of my way, peasant' mode. The reply is usually one of the signals we described earlier, which need an open window and a couple of fingers. Remember the requirement is to *'give signals correctly'*.

Indicators

We are discussing section 10 of the examiner's marking sheet – signalling. The great majority of signalling faults relate to use or improper use of indicators. These indicator faults usually fall into four categories.

1. Not giving a signal when one is necessary.
2. Failing to cancel a signal after use.

3. Signalling either too late or too early.
4. Signalling incorrectly (signal left and turn right, or vice versa).

Fault number one, when should you signal? Both *The Driving Test* and *The Highway Code* tell you to signal when to do so would assist or inform other road users, but there is a lot of misunderstanding over this point. If you are moving out to the right to pass a stationary vehicle, or pulling up at the kerbside, what comes first? Mirror. Correct. Why look in the mirror? For two reasons. First, to see if it is safe to do whatever you propose to do, and second, to see if there is any other road user who needs to be told what you're going to do.

However, if the road is empty in front and behind, there is absolutely no need to signal for these moves. There is no one else involved. The same thing applies when moving away from the kerb. Now this is an important and often misunderstood point. Don't automatically put on a right signal when you are about to move away. **Look** – mirror and right shoulder check. Look ahead. Nobody in sight front or rear, so why signal? It's not necessary.

On the other hand if someone is coming up fairly close behind you it would be misleading to signal; just put yourself in his place for a moment. Imagine you are driving along and approaching a stationary car on your side of the road. As you approach it, on comes its right indicator. What is your reaction? You think 'Now is this idiot about to pull out in front of me or not? If he is, he ought to know better and if he isn't, why switch the signal on and confuse me?' The correct action is to wait until the road behind is clear, then move when there is no need to signal.

If, however, there is a vehicle approaching from your front, or one approaching from a long way behind you, then it certainly would be helpful to signal to either of these drivers before driving off.

If a vehicle is approaching from some distance behind you, you only signal and move away if it is sufficiently far away for you to pull out without causing it any danger or inconvenience. This point is covered by the section, *'move away safely'*.

So, don't signal unnecessarily when moving off, and don't signal when there are vehicles approaching from close behind you. Let them pass first and then you probably won't need a signal.

Please note: A signal must never be a substitute for a look in the mirror.

A signal must never be a substitute for a look in the mirror.

Many experienced drivers make this mistake. Giving a signal carries no right whatsoever to carry out any manoeuvre – the onus is always on the driver to first ensure that it is safe to do so.

Be quite clear over signalling or not signalling when moving away. You don't signal when there is traffic closely approaching from behind – you let them go.

So, we have seen that there are times when we don't signal when passing a stationary car, pulling up at the kerb, or when moving away from the kerb.

However, don't confuse these three moves with turning into or out of a side road. **When turning at a road junction we always signal, even though the mirror shows no traffic behind.** Why? Well we signal for the benefit of anyone we might meet at the road junction. We probably cannot see into the road we are joining, so we don't know who might be approaching the junction on that road, so unless visibility is unusually good, we always signal when turning at junctions. The diagram makes this clear.

Car A is approaching the T junction and can't yet see car B. When he does see car B, he will immediately benefit from the left signal given by B, and realise that B is turning into the side road and not passing down the main road in front of him.

Although there is no following vehicle, A has signalled his intention to turn LEFT at the junction. Although they cannot yet see each other, car C will benefit from the knowledge that A proposes to turn left; it does away with the possibility that A might try a very swift turn to the RIGHT, so endangering car C.

The question of whether or not to signal depends on the situation and the driver's thoughts and assessment. The operative word here is 'thought'.

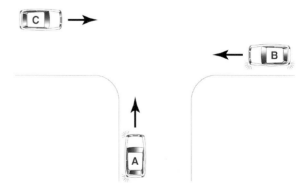

This is where giving a signal differs from a look in the mirror – mirror should be automatic. Don't over-signal, or signal unnecessarily – the examiner would soon realise that you are not giving any thought to your signals.

Item 2 in indicator faults is failing to cancel a signal after use. Your mechanical knowledge tells you that a simple ratchet device at the top of your steering column will cancel a signal you have given after you have turned and then straightened the steering wheel.

It is necessary, however, to turn the wheel through a quarter of a turn or so, for the signal to self-cancel. Sometimes, for example when you have left-signalled to pull up by the kerb, you don't turn the wheel sufficiently to operate the self-cancelling gadget. It is all too easy to forget to cancel the signal by hand so when you move away again you move off to the right with a left signal still flashing, and that will fail you for sure.

I am sure you can imagine various circumstances in which uncancelled signals can be dangerous.

It is every driver's responsibility to see that signals are cancelled either automatically or manually, immediately they have served their purpose. **You** switched it on, **you** see that it's switched off, or pay the price.

Fault number 3 is signalling too late or too soon. Remember the examiner is looking for signals 'properly timed'. If he asks you to take the second road on the right, and you immediately put on a right signal, you then give the impression that you are taking the first turning. Misleading and dangerous.

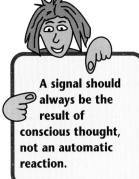

A signal should always be the result of conscious thought, not an automatic reaction.

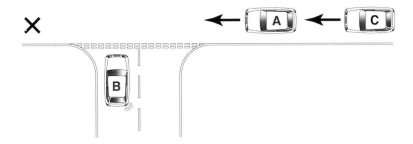

Another easily made mistake on signal timing is as follows: You are in car A. Car B is at the junction waiting to move off and turn right. Car C is following you, and you propose to pull up at point X. If you put on a left signal at the point where car A is located in the diagram, you tell car C you are going to do something, although he doesn't know what, but car B will completely misread your intentions and assume you intend to turn left at the junction. Unless he is unusually cautious, he could start to move out, right in front of you. A dangerous situation resulting from your signalling too early.

You should of course have delayed your signal until you were level with car B. Better still, is this not a case for the open window and the 'slowing down' arm signal as well? Both B and C would see the signal and realise your intentions immediately.

Signalling too late can be as bad as signalling too soon. A signal is intended to warn other road users of what you propose to do, not confirm what you are already doing. How often one sees experienced drivers giving a signal which is far too late to be any use to others.

Junctions with traffic lights are favourite locations for this bit of thoughtlessness. A car will stop at the red traffic-lights in the right hand lane, but only when the lights turn green will he signal his intention to turn right. By then he has a string of cars behind him also in the right lane, who assumed he was going straight ahead. Because of opposing traffic, all he can do is move out to the centre of the junction and wait, and all those behind him are stuck there. Ill mannered and thoughtless. He should have signalled a right turn on approaching the junction.

Fault number 4, signalling incorrectly, often occurs in connection with roundabouts. I don't propose to deal at length with how to tackle roundabouts, but we will go through the common signal faults. Top of the list must be the character who intends to go straight ahead at the roundabout – usually taking the second exit – but actually signals '**right**' on approaching. This right signal is changed to a **left** just before leaving the roundabout, and this last part is quite correct.

Why the **right** signal on approach though? The majority of roundabouts are really crossroads, two major roads crossing each other. Others of course have additional roads joining and then it gets a bit more complicated. You would not signal right at a crossroad when you intend to go straight ahead, so why do it at a roundabout?

The only time a right signal is given at a roundabout is **when you are going further round to the right than straight ahead**, or further round than 180 degrees, or 12 o'clock, however you wish to put it. The following two diagrams illustrate this.

Figure 1

Figure 2

In figure 1 it is only necessary to signal **left** at point A, just prior to leaving the roundabout.

In figure 2 the car is going further round than 12 o'clock, so a **right** signal is given on approach, changing to a **left** at point B, just before the exit.

If, on approaching a roundabout the examiner asks you to take the second exit from the roundabout, don't immediately switch on your left signal. You would be giving other road users the impression that you were taking the first exit.

So we can see that signals need a lot of intelligent consideration. They should not be just a reflex action.

Do I need to signal in this situation?
What signal is required?
When should I give the signal?
Shall I be making my intentions absolutely clear?

A final point on incorrect signals, and this can arise from misinterpreting the examiner's instructions.

Suppose you are asked to take the next turning on the left. The words don't quite sink in, because a noisy lorry went past, you were concentrating hard on your driving, you were a bit tensed up or whatever. You check the mirror, switch on a right indicator, move over to the right and start to slow down. Down into second gear, then just before turning right you realise he had asked you to turn left. Panic. Horror. What should you do?

Only one thing you can do. You turn right, safely and correctly. Do not under any circumstances attempt to turn left. You have signalled and positioned for a right turn, so turn right. You can always apologise to the examiner.

No one ever failed through taking a wrong turning provided the turn was correctly carried out. However signalling **left** and

Once you have signalled and positioned for a given manoeuvre don't change it to something else half way through.

turning **right**, or vice versa, is an accident in the making, no doubt of that, and of course is instant failure. I cannot emphasise enough that: Once you have signalled and positioned for a given manouevre don't change it to something else half way through even if it means turning round further on and coming back. Changing your mind half way through a turn can be desperately dangerous.

Incidentally if you do have some difficulty with left and right, it is not a problem on the test. More people suffer from this than you imagine, and it is often worse when under pressure.

It is in fact a mild form of dyslexia and nothing to be alarmed about or ashamed of. Your examiner will be quite used to the symptoms, and if you are a sufferer, tell the examiner or ask your instructor to tell him that you do have a bit of difficulty with left and right. The examiner will help you with turnings, and if he sees that you do indeed tend to muddle left and right, he will do everything possible to make his directions clear. He will probably point in the required direction in addition to giving verbal instructions.

Bear in mind though that *nothing* excuses signalling one way and turning another.

Hand Signals

These are more correctly called arm signals, since a partly open window and a hand peeping out from the wrist downwards, with fingers wriggling coyly, doesn't convey much to other road users.

At one time, test candidates were required to make use of arm signals during the driving part of their test, but this was dropped in 1976. However, the syllabus for the written theory test includes knowledge of hand signals and they are described in the current *Highway Code*; make sure you know them. Today's driving conditions can produce situations where an arm signal would be appropriate.

All signals are intended to warn and inform other road users and an example of a useful arm signal would be on approaching a zebra crossing, where a hesitant pedestrian hovers by the kerbside.

As you approach and slow down, your brake lights warn **following** traffic of your probable intentions. If a 'slowing down' arm signal is used in addition, this is also seen by any **oncoming** traffic, plus the pedestrian, neither of whom can see your brake lights.

There are not many occasions when an arm signal and indicators are used together at a turn. One example is when you want to make a right turn where there are two or three small side roads close together. You would do your **mirror**, **signal**, **position**, **speed** and **gear** drill, using the indicator signal prior to moving over to the right to position yourself for the turn. At this point it would be a good idea to use a right turn arm signal as you approach the turning you want, to make your intention clear.

To end this little section on arm or hand signals, I'll tell you of a really foolproof way to fail your test. A surprising number of learners don't know about this, which is why so many drop into the trap if the situation arises.

You know – or you should know – about your responsibility in the following scene.

If a pedestrian is walking along a road and comes to a side road leading off, then they have obviously got to walk across the end of that side road. If vehicles are either turning into or out of the side road, as cars A and B in the diagram, then they **must stop and give way to the pedestrian once he/she has started to cross.**

Just putting one foot into the road constitutes 'started to cross', and vehicles must give way.

Test candidate approaches T junction, in car A. Pedestrian steps off the kerb to cross. Our well taught learner stops the car to give way. The pedestrian then sees the car (probably for the first time), and decides not to cross, so stands in the gutter and waits.

Car is waiting for pedestrian, pedestrian is waiting for car. Stalemate. Anxious to please both examiner and pedestrian the candidate waves the pedestrian across with courtly sweep of his hand **and at that point fails his test**.

He fails under this section (10), '*give signals correctly*'. Unfortunately I have known this to happen many times The point here is that it is not up to any driver to wave a pedestrian across the road. That decision must be made by the pedestrian.

If you wave him on, quite prepared to sit and wait while he moves, and another car comes either past you or from the opposite direction (as car B), and clobbers your pedestrian, you are in deep trouble.

The unfortunate victim's next of kin have got you securely by the short hairs, because he was in the road **at your direction, on your signal**.

Now of course this situation does arise quite often, So how do we deal with it? We realise that two stationary road users both waiting for the other to do something can soon bring the area to a total standstill. The examiner is looking at you, the pedestrian is looking at you and you are looking at the pedestrian. So what happens next?

There are several ways to persuade the reluctant pedestrian to move. First, try to make eye contact; at least he knows you have seen him. You can then make a show of taking your hands off the steering wheel. A smile, a nod, one of these usually works. You can wiggle your ears if need be, but under no circumstances should you wave him on.

If he retreats to the footpath from where he started, fine; you can move on, but as long as he is actually standing in the road he has 'started to cross' and it remains his priority. In this case there is only one course open to you. You are discouraged from talking to the examiner while you are driving, but there's nothing to stop you talking to yourself. What I would do now is say 'now it's the pedestrian's priority' (not right of way – priority), 'but he obviously doesn't intend to cross while I am here, so I'm going to move on carefully, and get out of his way'.

The examiner knows then that you are aware of who should be doing what, and you have made a sensible decision. You have in fact displayed good manners and common sense.

Don't wave other road users on; this goes for pedestrians, cyclists, or other drivers. Let them make their own decision. No incorrect signals.

Flashing headlights

What a lot of misunderstanding there is on this one. A flashed headlight is very often given as a signal in two separate situations. One is a 'thank you' to another driver who has stopped to let you come through a narrow gap. The other is to indicate to an oncoming vehicle that you propose to hang back to let him come through the gap first. The second one is probably the most common. It's a sort of 'after you mate'.

These two signals are effective, they are in everyday use, and they are widely practised, but **they are unofficial**. *The Highway Code* quite clearly states that a flashed headlight has the same meaning as a toot on the horn, and that means 'I am here'. Nothing more. It is an unsatisfactory and confusing state of affairs.

Perhaps one day the signal will receive official approval, but I doubt it. In parts of the Continent of Europe a flashed headlight means the very opposite of our interpretation. They use it to say, 'You stay where you are mate 'cos I'm coming through there like a dose of salts'.

You can see that confusion between their version and ours could make for some expensive mistakes.

My advice is not to use a flashed headlight signal for any reason except to warn that you are there.

Now, think about this. You have a large lorry parked **on your side of the road**, 30 or 40 metres ahead. It's not a very wide road, and coming towards you is another car, about as far from the stationary lorry as you are. Clearly you are the one to give way, so you check the mirror and start to slow down. However the wife of the henpecked driver in the oncoming car says, 'Now George that's a learner coming. Stop and let the poor lad through'.

So George, bowed under years of bitter experience, promptly stops and gives you a quick flash of his headlights.

'Come on,' George is saying, 'I'll wait for you'.

Now George has stopped. His meaning is quite clear. Do you accept his invitation and go through or not? I have actually had a pupil who went through and was failed under exactly these circumstances. He was failed under section 11b of the test which says, '*take **appropriate** action* (my emphasis) *on signals by other road users*'. The examiner felt he should not have acted on an unofficial signal.

I have also had a pupil in similar circumstances who declined George's invitation and stopped. He was failed for '*undue hesitation*' (section 14).

I feel that the second examiner was correct in deciding it was a case of undue hesitation. The oncoming vehicle had stopped and made his intention quite clear. There is nothing so pointless as two stationary vehicles each waiting for the other. to make a move. The whole town comes to a standstill that way.

The first examiner, who awarded a major fault for accepting the invitation and moving on, was in my view both unrealistic and pedantic. The opposing car was stationary and had no following traffic; the situation was plain to see and it was a bad decision.

So this whole question of flashed headlights is a very grey area. Don't indulge in the practice yourself, and if you are given such a signal, think carefully about the circumstances. At the end of the day your decision must – as always – be based on good manners and **common sense**.

Hazard warning lights

These need little comment except to say that your instructor should tell you their purpose and how to operate them.

When in use, all four amber indicator lights flash on and off together – both sides, front and rear. They are used to draw attention to your vehicle if, for example, it has broken down, or you have unavoidably left it where it constitutes, a hazard. They are not in any way an excuse for the offence of parking in a no parking area.

At one time it was illegal to use them when on the move. That has now been modified to allow hazard lights to be switched on when approaching a hold up ahead, in order to warn following traffic of an impending obstruction. This applies only on motorways and derestricted dual carriageways. Make sure you know how to switch them on and off.

High intensity rear fog lights

These also need little discussion.

The theory test may well include a question on what precautions you would taken when driving in fog. It's all in *The Highway Code*, look it up. *The Highway Code* also has a section on lights, including fog lights. This says that fog lights (back or front) should only be used when visibility is down to 100 metres or less. This can be the result of fog, heavy rain, smoke or snow.

One sees drivers with both front and rear fog lights on when visibility is much greater than 100 metres, and this has a severe dazzling effect on other drivers. You must know this rule, and be ready to demonstrate how to operate the rear fog lights and, indeed, any other ancillary controls.

Brake lights

This is a signal which is given automatically whenever the footbrake is applied. Two or more red lights on the rear of the vehicle light up. If you are following another vehicle and his brake lights come on, you know immediately that he is braking, although you don't know how hard and you don't know if he intends to stop or only reduce speed.

When he begins to slow down you will see how sharply he is losing speed, and you can come to your own conclusions. When you are following another vehicle and its brake lights come on you should at once lift your foot off the accelerator and cover your brake pedal, ready to apply brakes if the vehicle in front is seen to be braking hard. In the same way, in a line of traffic, you can often see through the front and rear windows of the cars in front and see brake lights coming on in vehicles two or three ahead of you.

Tail-end shunts in lines of traffic are all too common, partly because drivers persist in driving too close to the vehicle in front, and because they fail to react to other vehicle's brake lights until it is too late. 'Tailgating' or driving too close to the vehicle in front is unquestionably the commonest single driving fault. Remember the 'two second' rule.

The examiner will expect you to react to brake lights on vehicles in front, and failure to do so can certainly fail you. Section 11(b) of the test says '*take appropriate action on **all signals** by other road users*'. Section 21 says '*Show **awareness and anticipation** of the actions of other road users*'. There is (my emphasis) that word anticipation again, which in turn is part of our quest for good manners and **common sense**. Anticipation **is** common sense.

Reversing lights

These, like brake lights, give you a clear signal. They are not controlled by the driver, they are white lights on the rear of a vehicle which are switched on automatically when reverse gear is engaged. Some small cars have only one reversing light and often only one rear fog light. In my view two of each should be mandatory, since when any one of these fails, it isn't always easy to be aware of it.

So, when the car in front stops and a white light or lights appear at the rear, you know he has engaged reverse. So what is he likely to do next? Go backwards – yes. Brilliant. Now you wouldn't think that was difficult to work out would you? You would be surprised how often this piece of deduction is quite beyond the average driver.

Look at the next diagram. Car A, driving from left to right, has been cruising round looking for a parking space and at last has found one. He stops a metre or so from the car at the front of the space and slightly in front of it, just as he was taught. He engages reverse gear and waits for car B to either pass him or hang back while he nips into his coveted space. The driver of car B fails to see A's reversing lights, or if he has seen them he has failed to grasp their meaning, so he stops close behind car A. By the time this dim-wit realises what A is trying to do, other vehicles have now piled up behind him, so he cannot reverse out of A's way. A has no alternative but to move on, abandoning the parking space he had spent ten minutes looking for. He is sorely tempted to give one of those special rude signals with the window open.

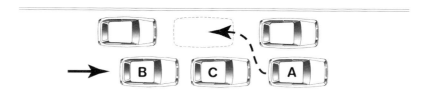

Tests have been failed in exactly this scenario, pupils of mine included. They have cursed themselves for their abysmal, total stupidity. It's a real gnashing of teeth and rending of garments job. At least it is in retrospect. At the time though, on test, under pressure, it's not difficult to get it wrong.

So this question of signals has more to it than you think. When you think of signals, most folk think of indicators, but there are these seven others as well. In fact there are even more than that.

With experience a good driver will suss out other drivers' intentions in many ways. The position in which a driver has put his car for example can often be a clue to his next move. Other drivers almost put out 'vibes'. In the diagram above, if he had had his wits about him, driver B would have spotted A's intentions even before his reversing lights came on.

We made the point earlier that good driving calls for many characteristics, not least of which is intelligent anticipation.

SECTION 11 OF THE TEST

Appropriate action on all signs and signals

In the previous section we dealt with the signals you give to other road users. Now we're going to deal with the signals which are given to you.

This section of the test contains five sub-sections. For a rather indifferent driver these five requirements probably offer more scope for disaster than any other section. You can make a real dog's breakfast of any of these five with very little effort. To get them right requires two things – good observation and a thorough knowledge of *The Highway Code*.

We'll look at each in turn, but you must realise that many hazards involve more than one of these five items. For example, a large junction can have traffic lights, plus traffic signs, plus road markings, plus signals given by other road users.

Traffic signs

Most traffic signs are located in a prominent and fixed position. Here's one that is not fixed and if you are not expecting it, it would be quite easy to miss. It's a round one and so gives a definite order which must be obeyed.

Can you identify it?

No it's not the coat of arms of the Family Planning Clinic, it's the sign attached to the business end of a lollipop lady's magic wand, and it must be obeyed. It spends most of the day stashed in the ladies' loo in the High Street, but comes out at the beginning and end of school times. It is important and it must be recognised and acted on when necessary.

Both *The Highway Code* and the excellent *Know your Traffic Signs* explain quite clearly how the shape and colour of signs tell you whether they are simply giving a warning or information, or give a definite order – either a 'you must' or a 'you must not'.

We made the point earlier that **you must learn your traffic signs and road markings** early on in your course of lessons. Too many learners leave it until the night before the theory test before swotting up this part of *The Highway Code*. This is a really naff attitude and can certainly fail you both your practical driving and the theory test.

Sadly, many experienced drivers never see an updated copy of *The Highway Code* once they have passed their test, and so are out of touch with more recent signs and road markings. Your safety, and that of other road users, depends on your thorough knowledge of the rules of the game, and that includes **all** traffic signs.

There is absolutely no excuse for any road user being in ignorance of any road marking or traffic sign. it amounts in fact to criminal negligence. Failure to act correctly on any traffic sign or road marking will automatically earn you a major fault from the examiner, and may also lead to a dangerous situation.

I think that's where we came in, and having got the lecture over, let's get back to traffic signs. Basically, to avoid test failure, you observe and act, where necessary, on all the signs, but we will go into a little more detail than that.

Do be very careful of 'STOP' signs. We have two in our small town, plenty of 'GIVE WAY' signs but only two 'STOP' signs. People fail the test over these from time to time, usually through one of two errors. The first is failing to actually stop; the candidate approaches slowly, has a very careful look in each direction still creeping slowly. Then, if the road is clear, they crawl out, gather speed and away. All done no doubt in perfect safety but they didn't actually stop and so contravened the sign, and broke the law in the process. It's a 3 points on your licence job.

The other common error at 'STOP' signs is to arrive at the junction and stop behind another vehicle which is waiting to emerge. When the road is clear, the car in front moves off, and you move off with him. This is quite wrong. When the car in front goes, you must move forward to the STOP line and stop again. Then look, and if the road is clear you may go. Each vehicle in turn must move up to the STOP line and halt. Your wheels must actually stop revolving, if only for a second.

It is perhaps not a bad idea, if you come to a 'STOP' sign, to briefly apply the handbrake, to confirm to the examiner your intention to stop completely.

Don't forget that speed limits are marked by traffic signs, and these are sometimes easy to overlook. Your test will very likely be along a route which involves more than one change of speed limit. Ask your instructor to explain clearly the significance of the small '40' or '50' signs, often found on lamp posts in built-up areas.

Watch carefully for 'SCHOOL' signs. Not all schools have the luxury of a lollipop lady, and we have already said that early morning, lunch time and mid-afternoon tests have school children as a major hazard.

Another one to look carefully for is the 'NO ENTRY' sign. Make sure you recognise it instantly – don't confuse it with the 'controlled zone' parking sign. (Look them up).

'NO ENTRY' signs will be found at one end of a one way street, the end at which vehicles may not enter. An examiner will not ask you to turn into a 'No entry' road in order to test your initiative. He will never direct you to do anything which is not in accordance with traffic laws, so don't have any worries on that score.

What he might do, however, is ask you to take the next **available** road on the left (or right). In this case, the next actual road could well be a 'NO Entry', so you give that a miss, and turn at the next one. Listen for the word **available**.

There is no need, at this point, for us to consider every sign. Ignoring any of them can lead to danger in some degree. The vital thing is for you to know and recognise them, and the other important thing is to actually see them in the first place. Wherever you are driving, and particularly in towns, you must have eyes everywhere. **Observation again**.

Road markings

Various traffic signs are combined with road markings –they go together. An example is the 'STOP' sign which we have just discussed. 'STOP' signs are placed on poles, clearly visible on approaching the junction, and are confirmed by road markings, as in the illustration.

'GIVE WAY' signs have a different marking, as in the second illustration – a double row of dotted lines as distinct from the thick, solid line at a 'STOP' sign. If you failed to see the 'STOP' sign on its pole, you should be able to tell the difference between a simple 'GIVE WAY' and a 'STOP' because of the different road markings.

A considerable amount of information plus actual instructions are painted on the surface of the road, and failure to take proper action on these markings is a major fault.

Arrows painted on the road in traffic lanes are most important, they show which lane you should be in depending on where you are going. The right hand lane in a road approaching a junction might be solely for traffic turning right at the junction, or it might be for both right turning and straight on traffic. The arrows will tell you. I even know of junctions where, because of the local layout, the left hand lane is actually for turning right! These lane markings guide the stranger to the town, but of course local knowledge gives any driver a considerable advantage.

See the illustration of lane markings in section 17 on page 140.

While dealing with lanes let me remind you that where a road is divided into lanes, you must drive in between the lane lines. Having part of your car in one lane and another part in the lane alongside will surely fail you.

The road markings follow after the traffic signs in *The Highway Code*. Learn them thoroughly, early on in your driving course. They are a great aid to safe driving. Have you ever noticed what a variety of lines there is down the middle of the road? Look them up and learn them, they tell you a lot about the road you're on.

Traffic lights

Too many tests are failed at traffic lights because drivers allow themselves to be caught unawares. If you see a set of green traffic lights two or three hundred metres ahead, don't assume that they will still be green when you get there. Better to assume they will have changed to red and start making your plans to stop at the right place.

The first essential is to learn the sequence of colour changes so that whatever colour or colours are showing when you first see a traffic light, you instinctively know what comes next.

Remember after green comes amber, which only lasts two or three seconds, and is followed by red. Amber does not mean dash across as quickly as possible, leaving the driver three cars back to do the decent thing and stop. Amber means '**stop if it is safe to do so**'. This means that as you approach, if the green turns to amber, you stop unless (1) you are too close to the stop line to pull up safely, or (2) you are travelling too fast to pull up safely, or (3) you are being too closely followed by another vehicle.

So, as you approach the green lights, they change to amber. This is where you have to react quickly. Do you stop or not? We have just seen that much depends on what is behind you and how close it is. I suggest that it's a bit late to start finding out about this now – you should already have this information and so be ready to either stop or keep going.

It's obvious therefore that as you approach a traffic light, **even if it's green, you should check your mirror and see what is behind you**, so if you are faced with a short-notice stop, you have all the information you need.

No one close behind, so you stop. You are now probably the first vehicle in the line waiting for the lights to turn green again. In this situation you should be sitting with your handbrake on, but with **1st gear engaged**.

A split second has been defined as the time between the lights turning green and the taxi behind sounding his horn. If you are the first in the line and the lights turn green, you should be ready to **go**. It's a bit late at this point to start ferreting about in the gearbox for something suitable.

If you are three or four vehicles from the front of the line, by all means select handbrake on and neutral gear, then you can rest both feet. You have time enough to select 1st gear when you see the lights turn green. I have known more than one test failed, however, because a candidate held up other traffic as a result of being first in the line and not ready to move off when the traffic lights changed to green.

As a general rule, whenever you have to stop for more than a few seconds, it is a good idea to select neutral, having first applied the handbrake, and you can then give your feet and legs a rest.

In this connection let me offer you a cautionary tale with a moral, one which left your humble scribe with egg all over his face.

I had driven into town one wet, dismal morning and had to stop behind a battered old VW Beetle, which was waiting at a pedestrian crossing for an elderly couple to totter across. I noticed the VW was fitted with a towbar, surmounted as usual by a 50 mm towball. I wondered idly what one towed behind a Beetle. A Mirror dinghy perhaps or an adapted baby buggy?

I sat there, in first gear, **handbrake off**, ready to go. It was a wet day you remember. Without warning my wet shoe slipped off the clutch. The car leapt forward and just before the engine stalled, we dealt the little Beetle a teeth-rattling smack up the bum. I watched, mortified, as the door of the VW slowly opened and out got the biggest, ugliest, hairiest-looking feller I had ever seen. How he got into the car in the first place, God knows.

His hands seem to hang level with his knees as he shambled slowly towards me and I decided I would at least greet him standing up. I got out, convinced that one wallop from him and I could be maimed for life.

'I'm terribly sorry,' I grovelled. 'Entirely my fault, my foot slipped off the clutch and …'

He actually smiled as he surveyed the two vehicles coupled, as it were, in some sort of automotive mating ritual. 'I shouldn't worry,' he said, 'It doesn't seem to have done mine any harm.'

He began to retrace his steps. I followed him, gabbling. I offered my name and address, insurance details, Swiss bank account number – anything, all of which were declined with an airy wave. He shovelled himself back into his little car and took off in a series of jerks, the first of which produced a depressing, metallic rending noise from the front of my car.

I surveyed the havoc wrought by his towball on my front end and drove on, a sadder and wiser man. The mess eventually cost several hundred quid to put right, so you can see why I am not really into sitting behind other vehicles in gear and without handbrake.

Another traffic light feature which occasionally causes problems is the addition of a green arrow to the standard round red, amber and green lights, as in the two illustrations below.

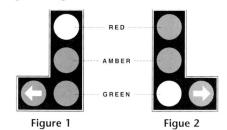

Figure 1   Figue 2

Figure 1 shows a filter arrow. When the red light is showing plus the green arrow pointing left, the green arrow allows vehicles to turn, or 'filter', to the left. At the same time, vehicles wishing to go straight ahead or turn right are controlled by the red light, and must remain stationary. When the red light changes via red/amber to green, the green left facing arrow disappears leaving only the normal round green light. When this shows, traffic may of course proceed in any direction, left, right or straight ahead.

Figure 2 is not strictly speaking a filter arrow. The right facing arrow fulfils a different purpose from the left facing filter arrow. In this illustration the round green light has the usual meaning i.e. that traffic may go, providing it is safe, in any direction; left, right or straight ahead. The addition of the right facing green arrow signifies that there will be no oncoming or opposing traffic, therefore vehicles wishing to turn right can do so in the knowledge that there will be no need to wait in the centre of the junction. **There will be no oncoming traffic to give way to; they will have a red light.**

Often this right-facing arrow does not light up until the round green light has been showing for some time, and during this time traffic will be flowing in both directions. When the green right facing arrow lights up, the oncoming traffic will get a red light and stop. It is then possible to make your right turn without the need to give way to opposing vehicles.

Junctions with traffic lights which have these additional arrows are quite common, but they do cause test failure where they are not fully understood. An example could be as follows.

If you come to a junction with traffic lights as in figure 2, and you wish to make a right turn, if the green light is showing but not the green arrow, you treat it as an ordinary traffic light. You move out to the centre of the junction and wait there, if necessary, for oncoming traffic. If there is then a gap in the opposing traffic and it is safe for you to make your right turn and go, then do so. **You do not need to wait for the green arrow.**

Remember the round green light tells you that you may proceed in any direction you wish provided it is safe to do so. The later appearance of the right facing green arrow merely tells you that there will now be no more opposing traffic to which you must give way.

If you wish to make a right turn at a junction with traffic lights, with or without this right facing arrow, the procedure is simple. Assuming you are the first vehicle in the queue at the red light, you will be waiting in the right hand lane with a right indicator showing. When the lights turn green you must move out into the centre of the junction and wait there while giving way to opposing traffic.

If opposing traffic prevents you from turning right immediately, you should **not wait behind the stop line**. You must move out to the centre when the green light shows. If you don't, and there is a long string of opposing traffic, you may well be still waitng behind the stop line when the lights turn back to red; then you have to wait and go through the whole process again.

By this time the driver behind will no doubt be trying to get a message across with his horn. So move out to the centre so that two or three other vehicles can move out behind you, and if you are still there when the lights return to red, this will stop any further opposing traffic, **and you can then complete your turn**. Any vehicle which has moved out with you will also move away, but any vehicle which is still behind the stop line when the lights return to red will have to wait until they turn green again.

If you are following another vehicle which intended to turn right at a junction such as this, when it moves out into the centre of the junction and then waits for opposing traffic, **you move out close behind it**. Waiting behind the stop line, or in other words failing to move forward when the lights are green, is quite a common cause of test failure. It causes delay and inconvenience to other road users, and constitutes a major fault.

So then, don't jump amber or red traffic lights. Amber means 'stop if it's safe to do so'. Don't let traffic lights catch you with your pants round your ankles. Whatever colour or colours are showing as you approach, immediately remind yourself of what comes next and be prepared for them to change as you approach. Be ready to take appropriate action, and check your mirror as you anticipate the next probable action.

Finally when the lights are green in your favour don't zoom across the junction looking straight ahead. **Look left and right.** A green light only has one meaning, it means it's your turn. It doesn't guarantee that it is safe to go. Taking effective observation at a junction applies just as much where a traffic light is involved as it does for any other junction.

I have failed pupils on mock tests for behaving like a horse with blinkers on at junctions, and the examiner will do the same. Green light or not – **look both ways at all junctions**.

Signals by traffic controllers

Authorised traffic controllers means police officers, traffic wardens and (in school crossing situations only) lollipop ladies or men. Traffic control signals given by police officers and traffic wardens are illustrated in *The Highway Code*. You must learn them and be prepared to act on them at any time. They are also included in the theory test. A supervised school crossing is directed by a lollipop person (or School Crossing Patrol). We saw the sign used to control traffic illustrated on page 85 – under 'Traffic Signs' and this sign, when used by the crossing warden, has the full weight of the law behind it, in just the same way as a signal from a police officer. So spot them, slow down and be ready for their next move. **Anticipation.**

In addition to signals by authorised people you may well find traffic being directed by a stand-in. At the scene of an accident or temporary road works where single line traffic is necessary, someone may have taken charge of the situation, be it another motorist or a council workman complete with fag end and wellies. It is obviously sensible to comply with the signals given, however inexpertly – Remember good manners and common sense.

Signals by other road users

The most frequent signals from other vehicles are those given by indicators. Given clearly and in good time they are a very great benefit to other road users. Sadly they are not all given in this way. When you see an indicator on another vehicle, immediately try to anticipate his next move. Will he slow down? Will he take up a position in the road consistent with what you think he's going to do next? Yes – both these seem logical.

Watch for any move which does not seem to fit in with the signal. If the car in front signals left and then moves out to the right, he has either given the wrong signal or is positioning himself badly for the proposed turn. On the other hand maybe he has moved to the **right** to negotiate a very tight turn into a narrow entrance on the **left**. We're not sure – yet. Until we are, let's hang back until his intentions are more clear. Look at the following diagram.

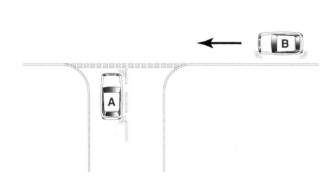

I had a pupil who was in this situation on test. He was in car A waiting to emerge at the T junction and turn right. The main road to his left was clear and car B was signalling a left turn into the side road from which A was emerging. Accordingly, my pupil started to move off and turn right. Immediately the examiner used the dual controls and stopped the car. Had he not done so, car B would probably have killed them both.

The examiner had realised a vital fact which my pupil had failed to spot, i.e. that car B was travelling far too fast to make the left turn. He had in fact no intention of turning left, he had failed to turn off his left indicator, having used it on a previous occasion, and he was travelling much too fast to be able to stop if my pupil had emerged.

The pupil had taken the signal at face value without giving it much careful thought, and he was quite rightly failed under section 15 of the test for emerging without effective **observation**. A useful lesson learnt.

In circumstances like these do be very careful about these 'left' signals. Be a bit suspicious, wait a while until you have further evidence of the other driver's intentions to turn left. Wait until he begins to slow down, then perhaps you can believe the signal.

In the previous chapter we listed all the different ways in which one road user can signal to another, indicators are not the only signals by any means.

Watch for the other signals. Watch particularly for the lorry with the hazard warning lights flashing, he is probably unloading therefore stationery for some time. Tests have been failed by candidates stopping close up behind just such a vehicle, the candidate having failed to see the hazard warning lights or realise why they were in use. If other traffic piles up behind you in these circumstances, it's another 'egg on the face' situation.

We saw in the reversing lights section how it is important to react to the other driver who is trying to reverse into a parking space. Similarly with other vehicles' brake lights – all these signals are there to keep you both informed and warned, to help you anticipate other drivers' intentions.

Finally a word or two about signals given by emergency vehicles. These include fire and rescue vehicles, ambulances, police vehicles and, less commonly, Coast Guard and bomb disposal vehicles. If you hear sirens or two-tone horns, try to locate where they are, maybe coming towards you, maybe catching up from behind. Look for flashing blue lights.

Don't over react. If the emergency vehicle is catching up from behind, the driver does not want you to come to a shuddering standstill. Keep well into the left to give him every chance to overtake. Slow down perhaps if you are approaching a narrow section of road or possibly a refuge in the middle of the road. Make it as simple as possible for him to overtake you. Again, **good manners** and **common sense**.

On this subject of emergency vehicles may I warn you of a rather unusual cause of test failure. My pupil was driving along a main road and saw an ambulance waiting to emerge from a side road on the left. In deference to the ambulance she stopped to let it emerge and was failed for undue hesitation, not making adequate progress. She was outraged by this quite correct decision on the part of the examiner and sobbed bitterly to me about the injustice of it all. I could imagine how she felt but I had to remind her that an emergency vehicle which is not on an emergency call is just another vehicle. No sirens or blue lights – no special treatment.

'You wouldn't have stopped for a milk float' I told her, 'Why the ambulance? The driver was probably going for dinner'.

A bitter pill to swallow but another lesson learnt, unfortunately the hard way.

Acting correctly on signals given by other road users also ties in closely with section 21 of the test. This calls for you *'to show awareness and anticipation of the actions of other road users'*. More of that when we get to it, but the key words in this driving business at all times are **observation** and intelligent **anticipation**.

SECTION 12 OF THE TEST

Care in the use of speed

On the subject of speed you must understand one basic but often forgotten fact. Whatever the speed limit is on your road, 20 mph, 70 mph or whatever, it does not automatically follow that it is safe to actually drive at that speed. **Any speed limit is just that, a legal maximum limit – not a recommended minimum.**

A Department of Transport road safety campaign some years ago had as its theme 'Speed Kills'. That is not strictly true. It is speed at the wrong time and in the wrong place which has tragic consequences. There are many situations in which 20 mph would be dangerously fast, in other circumstances 50 mph could be considered dawdling. Both of these are grounds for test failure.

A wide variety of conditions can call for a reduction in speed. Apart from suicidal ladies with prams, demented cyclists and similar moving hazards, varying road conditions can prompt a reduction in speed. A simple change in road surface is enough, pot holes, loose gravel etc.

Weather conditions, wet or greasy roads, fog, mist, ice, snow, heavy rain etc. etc. Heavy traffic, animals, road works, school children, your vehicle's load, any number of factors can affect your speed.

Although you may be driving at less than 30 mph you will certainly earn a major fault if your speed is not prudently matched to all the circumstances. This is one of the two common reasons for failure under this section.

The other fault is when passing from an area with a higher speed limit into a lower limit, and failing to see the signs or failing to act on them sufficiently promptly. It is no good passing the '30' sign at 50 mph, and then lifting off the gas pedal. That way you will be well into the 30 mph area before your speed is actually down to the correct level.

Police radar speed traps are often only a short distance into a '30' area (or 40 or whatever). They are not interested in the fact that you were in the process of slowing down, only in your speed when they actually clock you.

In the same way, the examiner will expect to see you doing 30 mph as you pass the '30' sign. The police may well give you a 10 per cent benefit of the doubt allowance. The examiner will not, and 30 means 30 as indicated on your speedometer. Very many of our existing speed limits are unrealistic and long overdue for review, but even when the limit seems unreasonable and other vehicles are overtaking you, the examiner will not condone your breaking the law and will give you little or no latitude in this area.

Recognise this sign?

One of the more widely disregarded traffic signs, its shape tells you that it is purely an advisory or warning sign, not a mandatory sign to be obeyed in all circumstances.

The local council scatter these signs about like confetti when they put tar and loose chippings on the road. In our part of the world the signs are often put out a couple of days before the work starts. Worse than that, they never bother to recover them when the job's done.

The signs are often made of paper and cardboard and so are biodegradable, and in due course they blow down or fall over and eventually rot. The result of all this is that the signs are completely ignored by most drivers, because they are not actually relevant throughout most of the time they are displayed.

Loose chippings are however a frequent cause of broken windscreens and when first put down can be quite dangerous. Most drivers with any sense at all are aware of the state of the road surface and react accordingly. But within a few days the chippings become ground into the road surface or swished to the side by traffic. The problem is soon over and 20 mph is no longer necessary, but the signs seem to remain for weeks.

Why on .earth am I rambling on about this, you ask. Well this book is about the reasons people fail the test, and believe it or not there are recorded instances of candidates failing the test through failing to strictly observe implicitly this advisory 20 mph. History does not tell us whether the tests concerned were carried out before, during or even long after the road works. One thing is for sure, either the candidate or the examiner was woefully short of common sense on the day in question. So, you have been warned: if you come across a temporary speed limit sign, use your common sense but err on the side of caution.

A later section, section 18, requires you to leave adequate clearance for *stationary vehicles*, and the question of speed is closely tied up with this. Put briefly, the less space you are able to allow between your own and a stationary vehicle, the lower your speed must be.

When we are considering circumstances under which we should reduce speed, passing close to stationary vehicles should certainly be one of them.

There are two golden rules which will not only help you to pass your test, but also to keep you accident-free in years to come.

The first rule is **always to travel at a speed at which you can stop in the distance you can see to be clear**.

This is particularly relevant in fog or any other form of poor visibility. Learn your stopping distances for various speeds and for different types of road surface. Learn what these distances look like, since there is no point in reciting, parrot fashion, that at 40 mph you need 36 metres (120 feet) in which to stop, if you have no idea what 36 metres looks like.

Remember also that at **any** speed, your stopping distance on a wet road is **doubled**. A stopping distance at a given speed, and the effect of a wet road are both likely to be theory test questions.

The second rule concerns your awareness of your distance behind the vehicle in front, having regard to the speed at which you are travelling. There are a couple of simple but effective means of keeping a safe distance.

One is to allow one to one-and-a-half car lengths for every 10 mph of speed, and the other is always to be at least two seconds behind the car in front.

You would probably be surprised at how far you travel in two seconds at only 30 mph. In fact you cover nearly 30 metres (90 feet) in two seconds, even at this low speed.

It is without doubt the most common serious driving fault on our roads today. I'm talking about driving too close to the vehicle in front, having regard to the speed at which you are both travelling. It has of course always been something for which examiners would watch, but as from 1993 it forms a separate section on the marking sheet. It is section 13 and we will look at that next.

Just going back to this rough rule of thumb, ask your instructor to explain and demonstrate to you the leaving of so many car lengths between you and the chap in front, and also the question of always being two seconds behind him.

To close this chapter on speed it might be appropriate to offer you another definition of good driving. We already know about it being a mixture of good manners and common sense. It also means being in the right place on the road at the right time, **at the right speed for the circumstances** and in the right gear for that speed.

This part of the examiner's marking sheet, section 12, exercising *'proper care in the use of speed'* means just that. It's not just about obeying the speed limit. It means adjusting your speed to the situation you happen to be in. That's what is meant by the right speed for the circumstances.

SECTION 13 OF THE TEST

Keep a safe distance behind vehicles

This has always been a feature of a candidate's driving which an examiner has kept in mind, but only since 1993 has it constituted a separate section on the marking sheet.

It is an area of driving in which a learner probably does better than an experienced driver. Following another vehicle at a safe distance is down to basic common sense, but the more experienced a driver becomes, the more familiar he or she becomes with the task, and unfortunately familiarity breeds contempt. All too often common sense goes out the window, together with respect for the law, for the highway code and many forms of reasonable behaviour.

Without doubt, driving too close to the vehicle in front is the commonest single serious driving fault. Every year it causes enormous accident damage, the loss of many lives and countless horrific injuries.

Whenever there is a multiple pile-up on a motorway, some of these idiots are interviewed on television and the patter is always the same. 'What could I do? The bloke in front just stopped, I couldn't avoid him'. Yet it was his own choice to be driving dangerously close to the car in front.

It is unbelievable and at the same time it's pathetic. It was probably in mist or fog or snow or heavy rain, but they all go blindly along at 70 or 80 mph, ten or fifteen metres or so from the vehicle in front – and some of them actually on the telephone!

At 75 mph you need around a hundred metres in which to stop, something like the length of a football pitch, and that's on a dry road. All too often though the attitude is 'don't worry about me Sunshine, if you stop, I can stop'.

He can't. At 70 mph a fit, alert driver will travel over 20 metres between spotting danger and even *starting* to brake.

We mentioned earlier the need to know your stopping distances at various speeds and also to know what those distances look like. From these figures and also from using the 'two second' rule you can see that you need to leave a much greater distance between you and the vehicle in front at 70 mph on a dual carriageway, than you do in slow moving traffic.

Let's look again at the golden safety rule that is as true in fog, ice, rain or snow as it is on a warm dry, summer's day, and that says: always drive at a speed at which you can stop in the distance you can see to be clear.

To fit the requirements of this section you can put this the other way round and say 'always leave clear sufficient distance to enable you to stop from the speed at which you are travelling'.

Always drive at a speed at which you can stop in the distance you can see to be clear.

The examiner will have the requirements of this section in mind all the time you are on the move, be it at 10 or 60 mph. You must keep it in mind too, always.

If you are driving at a safe four or five car lengths from the car in front and some whizz kid overtakes you and fills the space, then drop back a little to be at a safe distance from him. Don't ride on his tail with your headlights flashing, this will only amuse him. Remember there is no better lesson than a good example.

It is all too easy when under the pressure of the test, and while concentrating on speed limits and traffic signs and giving signals and all the other things you have to think about, to forget this business of sensible positioning, but the examiner will be watching it all the time.

The guideline of **good manners** and **common sense** applies to this section as much as to any other.

SECTION 14 OF THE TEST

Making progress at the appropriate speed

We saw in Section 13 of the test that you can fail by either driving too fast or too slowly for the prevailing conditions.

It is a popular misconception that if you drive slowly, i.e. 'carefully', give way to all traffic and show exaggerated courtesy to everyone, you must pass your test. You won't.

In today's crowded towns and cities it is essential that you make adequate progress. Holding up following traffic unnecessarily is dangerous, it prompts impatient drivers to take risky chances to overtake you. This puts both them and others at risk, and the basic fault lies with you.

Having said this, let me emphasise that we are talking about moving at the legal speed limit, or indeed less if the conditions call for it. If you are doing 30 mph in a 30 mph area, you must not allow yourself to be hustled into exceeding the speed limit by a driver behind you. Let him overtake you and go.

I remember a middle-aged lady who had taken her test twice and was determined to pass at her third attempt. In my opinion she was well capable of doing so, but on the day, she failed again. She was determined to do everything correctly, her manoeuvres were good, mirror and procedure at junctions, everything was beyond reproach, but throughout the entire drive she never got above third gear and never exceeded 25 mph. She had tried too hard and forgot the need to '*make progress*'. She passed at the next attempt having learnt an essential lesson.

An occasion when candidates often fail through hesitating too long is when emerging from junctions. This point is stressed in

The Driving Test, in the section dealing with making progress, which says 'move off at junctions as soon as it is safe to do so'. So in the same way that you can fail through driving either too fast or too slowly, at junctions you can fail through either bursting out into the main road without proper observation, or for sitting there dithering when it is obviously safe to go.

Dithering takes various forms but boils down to two headings. In simple terms it consists of not driving fast enough when on the move, or of taking too long to move off when stationary.

Dealing with driving too slowly, we saw previously, that *depending on conditions* 20 mph could be dangerously fast and 50 mph could be classed as dawdling.

These circumstances include the nature of the road and its surface, the density of traffic (on foot or motorised), visibility, weather conditions, your own condition – tired, bored, hungry, stressed, etc. etc.

If you are driving in a stream of traffic which is moving at a safe and legal speed and you fall further and further behind the vehicle in front, this is an example of not making adequate progress. You would be frustrating drivers following you and prompting them to overtake you, thus causing an unnecessary hazard for oncoming traffic. Certainly a major fault.

Failing to overtake when safe and appropriate to do so is another example of failing to make adequate progress. Tests conducted in busy towns often do not call for any overtaking. Our local test routes however, frequently make use of a fast stretch of main road dual carriageway, where the national speed limit is 70 mph. Tests are frequently failed here through candidates catching up a heavy lorry or large load doing, say, 50 mph, and failing to make any attempt to overtake when it is safe to do so. The expression *'make progress'* really is self explanatory, and is often the cause of test failure when, from all other viewpoints, the candidate's standard of driving is good.

So much for moving at an adequate speed, let's now look at avoiding undue hesitation when moving away. Basically this means moving off without delay as soon as it is safe to do so.

Having moved off, accelerate positively up to your desired cruising speed and this will be governed by traffic conditions. Don't make the common mistake of hanging on too long in an intermediate gear before changing smoothly up to the next one. Too long in the low gears means you will over-rev your engine, make a lot of noise and consume large quantities of petrol. (This is covered on pages 36–39, under section 3, *'make proper use of gears'*).

The suitability of any speed, therefore, can only be judged in the light of prevailing conditions or circumstances

Not every instance of undue hesitation involves other road users, so there are occasions when it might only be judged a minor fault. How much dithering or time-wasting an examiner will accept is a rather variable and unknown quantity. The odd instance is one thing, quite another is the candidate who automatically applies the handbrake at every junction, before even looking to see if it was necessary to stop at all.

Here's an important statement for you. Whether you actually stop at a junction or hazard or not, and if not, how fast you actually emerge, depends largely on one important factor – **visibility**.

For example, if you're approaching a junction with a good clear view up and down the road you are joining before you actually join it, and you can see the road to be clear, then the last thing you need to do is to stop and apply the handbrake. This would just be an unnecessary waste of time. Do this a couple of times on your test and you will certainly have blown it. (We are of course assuming that the junction concerned does not involve a 'stop' sign. Stop signs are generally found at potentially dangerous junctions where the visibility is severely limited).

It is important, once you have become accustomed to driving in traffic and coping with junctions, that you do not develop the habit of approaching a junction, or indeed any hazard, with your mind in neutral, intending to arrive there, stop, take a look round and only then start to make plans.

You must be prepared to make a prompt decision based, as much as possible, on what you have learnt as you approach. As we have seen, it depends on how good or bad is the visibility.

Failure to observe and plan ahead inevitably leads to undue hesitation. Be ready to go as soon as the lights turn green. Be ready to go before the pedestrian has reached the other side of the crossing. There are dozens of examples, and once again they're usually down to common sense.

That just about covers the subject of hesitancy and lack of progress, and we could leave it there. However I know that many learners have a dread of 'driving fast' so if you will bear with me I think we should just discuss this question of speed a little further.

We must understand that our impressions of speed are relative. If you travel a motorway at 70 mph and then turn off and immediately enter a 30 mph area, you get the impression that you have almost stopped. By contrast, 30 mph achieved down a busy, narrow town road with cars parked on each side can seem dangerously fast, and probably is.

When I have a pupil who starts to get uptight at any speed over 40 mph, we try to find a nice wide, straight stretch of de-restricted main road, and gently encourage them to build up to about 60 mph. After a couple of miles of this, 40 mph seems very much easier to cope with, and the pupil usually admits to having quite enjoyed the faster spell. It's all relative.

It is only natural that a learner on the first lesson is anxious, if not actually frightened. After all it's probably the first time they have travelled, under their own control, at a speed greater than that of a bicycle. On the other hand there is always the boy (or girl) racer who has mastered the controls in a field with Uncle Fred and is convinced that all they need now is a couple of lessons on the road and they're ready for the test.

As an instructor and passenger I know I would much rather deal with a beginner who has a healthy respect for the potential dangers inherent in piloting a ton of metal at 30 mph, than the brash youngster who reckons he already knows it all, and wants to take all bends on two wheels.

I much prefer the former and so, believe me, does the examiner.

Caution is a natural product of intelligent, constructive thought. Intelligence is essential to good driving; no way can it be learned parrot fashion.

They say you can teach a monkey to drive if you've got enough bananas. It's not true. Conversely the person who knows no fear is not brave, merely 'thick' and usually totally lacking in imagination. Naturally, therefore, the intelligent learner is very wary of letting things get out of control, and an experienced instructor is well aware of this. It is why every good driving school car has dual controls – just in case!

You do, however, reach a point in your lessons where the speed thing begins to come into perspective. With some pupils it is sooner, or later, than with others. At this point you begin to grow rapidly in confidence, and this point usually marks two significant milestones in your learning.

The first is that your physical handling of the vehicle is beginning to become automatic, or instinctive. You find that you no longer have to think which pedal to press, or when to press it, or ask if you are in the right gear. Because the vehicle control is becoming sub-conscious, you now have more mental capacity to devote to what is going on around you, what other people are up to.

You actually have time to plan ahead, to anticipate. In other words you are beginning to fit naturally into the big mobile game of chess, and you are starting to move your piece around the board sensibly and instinctively.

The second milestone you reach about this time is your awareness that **you are at last driving the car, not the car driving you**, and that is a most important step forward. From here on you should be able to keep up with the flow of traffic, avoid hindering other road users, and be able to make decisions which enable you to move off promptly and safely.

And how long does it take to reach this significant goal? Well, I would say anywhere between a few weeks and several years. Remember we're all different. We are not all born with the same characteristics or abilities. Some are adventurous, others cautious. We all have different talents. Different people shine at different things; painting, cooking, metal work, music, computer hacking or skate boarding – whatever. We therefore take to driving with widely differing attitudes and rates of progress.

I remember my 'phone ringing for the third time during my evening meal (it's an occupational hazard).

The Voice enquired 'How many lessons will my 17 year old son need to pass his test?'

I could see the gravy actually congealing.

'Well, put it this way' I said, 'How many piano lessons would he need in order to win the Leeds Festival?'

'That's a bloody silly question' replies the Voice 'as it happens he's not musical'.

'Well he might have no aptitude for driving a vehicle either' I suggested. 'Let me have him for a couple of hours and I'll give you a reasonable clue, but over the 'phone your guess is as good as mine.'

'I never thought of it that way' said the Voice.

I fervently hoped that the lad in question had got a few more marbles than his dad. As it happened he had, and he picked things up quickly.

I have seen so many pupils become unnecessarily frustrated because they didn't become Michael Schumacher in six weeks.

'Sharon Hotpants in my class at school passed first time after only eight lessons, and I can't reverse round a corner yet without climbing up the kerb.'

Do not despair (Sharon is probably a pain in the butt anyway). We all have varying abilities and progress at different rates. If people are constantly overtaking you and the thought of going faster fills you with dread, be patient. Master each step thoroughly before tackling the next. Confidence will come and with it the ability to make progress and avoid hesitation.

If you are negotiating a road with vehicles parked on both sides, the bit of road in the middle is obviously fairly narrow. If there is an oncoming car you need to make a decision. Either it's wide enough for you to go through at the same time or it isn't. If it **isn't** wide enough but you decide to go for it, you fail under section 16 of the test *'Section 16 – 'meet other vehicles safely'*. If it is wide enough for both of you, but you hang back and dither, you fail under section 14, *'undue hesitation'*. It's a tough world.

Cheer up – you can't possibly expect to get this sort of thing right during your early lessons. As with getting used to speed, judging speed, using speed wisely, it all takes time, and it takes some pupils longer than others. Be patient.

SECTION 15 OF THE TEST

Correct actions at road junctions

There are five sub-sections to this part of the test, which together are your guidelines for correct behaviour at junctions. Quite a high number of test failures are down to this section as a whole, and very many urban traffic accidents occur at junctions through drivers getting one of the five points wrong, and particularly when turning right. Let's look at the five sub-sections in turn.

Speed on approach

When approaching a situation where you must give way, the later you leave your braking the harder you will need to apply the brakes. This in turn leads to a fairly rough, abrupt stop and this is a sure sign to the examiner that you had not planned sufficiently far ahead. It also means that you will still be braking when you ought to be easing gently into the correct gear for moving off again – probably first. This in turn means that you won't get the gear change done until after you have stopped, thus probably wasting more time at the junction than was necessary. In fact the whole operation would have been carried out more quickly and smoothly if you had slowed down earlier, found the correct gear and (if safe to do so) emerged without actually stopping.

Another common result of late braking is failing to stop at the 'give way' line, so the front of the vehicle is projecting out into the main road. In addition to failing to adjust your speed correctly on approaching the junction, you have now also failed to take correct action with regard to the road markings.

Late breaking at junctions is either the result of not planning your approach correctly on seeing the junction, or worse still, failing to see the junction until it is too late to take the correct action.

Remember when we looked at traffic signs and road markings, we saw that not all 'give way' junctions are marked with traffic signs. Many are only marked by actual road markings i.e. the double broken white line across the end of the road. In certain conditions these can be difficult to see until you are on top of them, although they are always preceded by (usually) five hazard lines down the centre of the road.

Do beware. Some minor road junctions can have no road markings or signs at all. Local knowledge is a great help with these, but on unknown roads you must always be wary and make sure you spot warning clues to a junction.

Junctions with neither road markings nor signs constitute a particularly dangerous hazard. Rarely, if ever, found on main roads, they are still found on housing estates.

No priorities are marked on the approach roads, and the only safe way to tackle these hazardous features is to slow right down and have a good look in each direction before emerging. You have got to work on the basis that as you arrive there is going to be some brainless pillock hurtling across at right angles to you, imagining that he has the priority – assuming he sees the junction in the first place.

If you get an unmarked crossroad on your test, **slow** and **look** – or fail.

So far we have talked about speed at junctions when you are on a minor road and approaching a major road. The same guidelines apply when we are turning off a major road onto a minor road. Normally, depending on circumstances you can turn into a side road rather more quickly than you can come out of it, and so as a general rule you tend to turn into side roads in second gear and emerge from them in first gear. This is a generalisation **not** an inflexible rule.

When approaching a side road which we wish to turn into, we must reduce speed down to a suitable level for second gear, and then change into second gear. (Don't change into second at 30 mph or more, use the brakes for slowing down, not the gearbox). Once again, if we leave the braking too late, the gear change will be too late and then we shall still be gear changing as we go round the corner, when we ought to have two hands on the steering wheel.

A junction or indeed any hazard needs to be approached at the right speed and the right position on the road, that's what this section is all about. To achieve this we need to go through a sequence of actions **in the right order and in good time**.

Remember this sequence?

MIRROR	SIGNAL	POSITION	SPEED	GEAR
M	S	P	S	G

(**M**ust **S**urely **P**revent **S**ome **G**rief)

We saw this **M S P S G** sequence earlier on page 38, dealing with correct use of gears. We've just used it again in connection with speed. It will continue to crop up, since it is used whenever a hazard is involved.

Observation

This really means **effective** observation. There is no point in looking up and down the road at a junction unless you absorb what there is to see, analyse it correctly, then decide on your next action based on what you have seen.

When we talk about emerging at junctions, beginners tend to automatically think about T junctions. True, these are the commonest form of junction, but the need for effective observation applies just as much at all junctions; crossroads, roundabouts and junctions with traffic lights. When we discussed traffic lights you remember we said that you still need to look both ways even though you have a green light, because, sadly, many drivers will jump amber and even red traffic lights. Obviously the examiner will not expect you to slow right down when you have a green light at a busy junction, but he will expect to see you having a quick but effective look in each direction.

At one time pupils were taught at junctions to look right, left and right again before moving away. In today's dense traffic conditions this routine is not enough. Watch a good driver at a busy junction – he looks as though he's watching the men's finals at Wimbledon. His head is turning left, right, left, right and left again, right up to the very moment he moves off, and then one more glance to the right as he actually begins to move.

On page 104, we saw that unnecessary delay or hesitation at junctions will cause failure. We're now talking about failure due to the exact opposite, i.e. bursting out at a junction without proper observation.

Our correct course of action lies somewhere in between these two extremes. So how do you pick the right moment to move off at a junction, without either dithering or speaking out of turn?

This is a question which worries many learners. Indeed many experienced drivers tend to manage by the seat of their pants rather than treating the task logically. It's a task which can be reduced to a simple formula, a drill if you like. It's logical and based once more on good manners and common sense.

Before making the decision to actually move, your sequence of actions must be as follows, beginning with the big O – **Observation. Look, assess, decide**, then finally **act**.

Now that's logical enough but the difficult part is the 'decide' bit. You must realise that you will not perfect this sequence, particularly including a quick decision, without a lot of practice.

Assume we arrive at a T junction and wish to turn left. We have a good view up the road to our right and there is no traffic approaching down the road we wish to join. Do we need to look to the left at all? Surely the traffic coming from our left will be over on the far side of the road we are joining – but will it?

Look at this diagram.

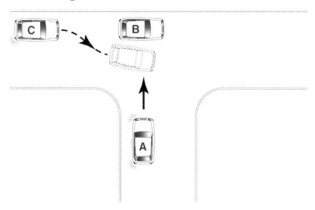

We are in vehicle A and about to turn left, but car B is parked on the opposite side of the main road, as shown. (If he knew the rules he wouldn't park opposite a junction, but he has done so.) Car C is coming from our left and as you see he will have to move out to pass the stationary car B, thus putting himself on our side of the main road. If we had emerged without the routine look to the left, a head-on situation would have resulted.

In a similar situation car B might be moving, with car C about to overtake him and this would give the same result as before. Again car C should not overtake when approaching a junction for this very reason, but it does happen.

Let's now take the same scenario, we are going to turn left on emerging from a T junction. This time there is no traffic approaching from the left so our prime concern is any traffic approaching from the right.

We have looked and seen an approaching vehicle. Now we assess the situation and decide whether to go or wait, i.e. act or not.

You are now face-to-face with the problem decision which bugs learner drivers probably more than anything else. Do we move out and go, or do we wait for the vehicle coming from the right? If we wait and let him go first, are we going to be marked for undue hesitation? If we move off and make our left turn are we guilty of emerging without effective observation?

Getting this right takes a lot of practice, believe me. There are drivers who have been at it for twenty years or more and still haven't got it right, so do not despair.

Isn't this one of the beginner's biggest worries? Of course it is, so let's look at it logically. It's not difficult and the principal guidelines are still **good manners** and **common sense**.

The decision you make must not be based on any sort of gut feeling or what your horoscope said this morning. In this situation you always use the following logical sequence or train of thought, and it will invariably point you to the correct solution.

You've seen the approaching vehicle, you've seen how far away it is and you've seen how fast it is travelling. Feeding this information into your mental computer will give you some idea of how long he will take to arrive at your junction, where you are both going to be wanting the same piece of road. This is the assess part of the process. Now you know how long before he arrives, you can answer the following four vital questions.

If I move out now will I make the other driver:
1. brake or slow down to avoid me?
2. steer, swerve or alter course to avoid me?
3. will I place him in any danger?
4. will I in any way inconvenience him?

In other words, if I pull out now will he have to do anything about it, and will it get up his nose?

Those four questions are the essential keys to the decision you make, i.e. to go or to wait. If all four answers are 'no' then you should be on your way, because if you aren't, then you are hesitating unnecessarily. If any one answer is a 'yes', then you wait. (It's probably 'yes' to the other three as well.)

In theory that's all there is to it. You now know exactly how to decide whether to emerge from a junction or wait for the other vehicle. In practice though, it's not quite that simple.

This four question business is straightforward and logical enough, I'm sure you will agree, but in fact the inexperienced driver will often see the approaching vehicle, ask the four questions but then unfortunately the answer to one or more may well be 'I don't know' or 'I'm not sure'.

Be of good cheer, because that has been provided for. There is a very good piece of advice that applies to life in general and driving in particular – advice which many a Mum has handed out to her daughter – and it is simply: **'If in doubt, don't'**. (Ring a bell, does it?)

So we did the **look** bit, that was no problem. We did the assess bit, and that was fairly straightforward. The bit we're hung up on is the **decide**, and that is not so simple. It does in fact take a lot of practice, particularly if the decision is somewhat border-line. Having **decided** we must of course act. You act on your decision, in other words you either wait for a more suitable opportunity to move, or you go, there and then, smoothly and without delay.

Asking these four questions may sound a bit long-winded but they are quite vital in making the correct decision every time. They take only a couple of seconds to run through your brain, and what they boil down to is 'if I pull out or across in front of this other chap, would he need to take any sort of avoiding action at all?' **If the answer is 'yes' then I would be absolutely in the wrong.**

This is the definitive standard by which you decide on your actions at any hazard which involves another road user, particularly when they have priority. Do it often enough and you will find that it becomes almost subconscious, or instinctive. It does, however, need a lot of practice before you can make the correct decision every time and without hesitation.

Look, assess, decide and act – just like that … Until you can do this at every hazard you are not ready to take your test.

LOOK, ASSESS, DECIDE and ACT.

Position before turning right or left.
Common errors before turning are:

1. swinging out to the **right** before a **left** turn,
2. swinging out to the **left** before a **right** turn.

Two (2) is often done **after** moving out to the centre of the road, in preparation for a right turn. The diagrams show both errors; the dotted line shows the *incorrect* course in each case.

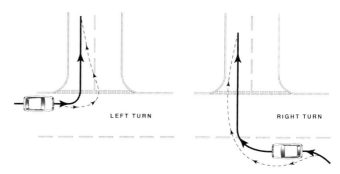

LEFT TURN   RIGHT TURN

These errors are particularly dangerous, since they involve a real danger of colliding with a vehicle which might be overtaking you either on your right or your left, depending on which direction you have signalled. Once you have signalled a turn, following vehicles are likely to overtake you as you slow down. If you signal left they will naturally overtake you on your right, as usual. If you signal a right turn and then take up the correct position for turning right, i.e. move out towards the centre of the road, then following traffic will overtake on your left, or nearside. Swinging back towards your left prior to a right turn thus poses a very real threat of a sideways shunt.

There is no need or excuse for a car to swing out in this fashion prior to turning, but it is often necessary for the driver of a long or articulated vehicle to do so. Do be prepared for this. If the big lorry in front of you signals a left turn and then moves out to the right, don't assume he has given the wrong signal, and start to overtake him on his left. You would find yourself jammed underneath his trailer when he actually does turn left.

Talking of big lorries, let's think about your correct position when emerging from a side road, and a long vehicle wishes to turn into that side road.

We all know that we should not cut right-hand corners, but a big lorry or a bus usually has to do just that in order to get round the corner.

In this next diagram the lorry cannot turn into your side road while you are in position A, at least not without tearing off a chunk of your offside front wing.

As you see him approaching from your left, signalling a right turn, then the sensible and courteous solution is for you to stop at position B. If however you are unable to see him before stopping at position A, he will want you to move away before he attempts to turn. In circumstances like these therefore, watch for his signal requesting you to emerge and be on your way, thus vacating the piece of road that he needs for his turn.

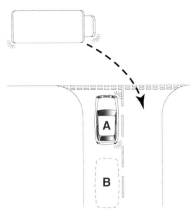

Don't just act blindly on his signal though, remember to take effective observation in both directions before moving off. The onus is on you to emerge into the main road **when it is safe to do so**.

Exactly the same problem would arise if the large vehicle were coming from your right, and wanting to turn left into your side road. He would need to take a wide sweep when turning left, and would need to use part of the road on which you are sitting while at the 'give way' line. Again, therefore, he would want you to move away before he attempted his turn.

Under certain circumstances then, some modified positioning will be called for at junctions, and as usual, **observation, good manners** and **common sense** are called for.

Your position at a junction, for example a crossroads with traffic lights, will depend on the direction you wish to follow at the junction, plus the relevant road markings.

On approaching such a junction it is essential that you decide which lane you need. Get in it and stay in it.

You must position your vehicle so that it is within the road markings which form the boundaries of your lane. If you wander so that most of the car is in the correct lane but part of it overflows into the adjacent lane you will certainly earn a major fault under section 11a of the test – *'take correct action on all road markings'*. You would also be at fault under section 17 of the test – *'position the vehicle correctly, **exercise lane discipline'***. (My emphasis).

We have already seen that it is usually more difficult and dangerous to turn right than left, but turning left can also have its problems. Look at the illustrations on the following page.

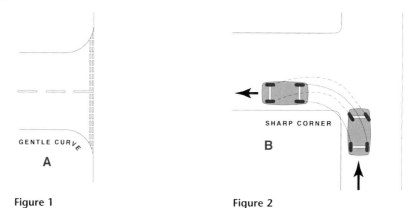

Figure 1   **Figure 2**

Which is the easier corner for a left turn? Not much doubt about it, corner A with its gradual curve is easier.

Your instructor should cover the subject of turning left at very sharp corners and explain to you how, on a vehicle which is turning, the rear wheels always follow a shorter path than the front ones. Figure 2 illustrates this and shows how one can all too easily have the nearside rear wheel riding up over the kerbstone.

The longer the vehicle, the more exaggerated is this corner-cutting effect with the rear wheels. Remember the bit about the large lorry having to swing out wide to the right before turning a left corner? This is the reason for it.

The problem is not nearly so pronounced with a small car but Figure 2 shows how easily one can mount the kerb with the rear wheel during a left turn at a sharp corner. It's a common enough fault which can have serious consequences. If you have a police-man standing on the corner with his mind in neutral and his thoughts on lunch, he's going to be a bit put out if you run over his toes. Seriously, a mother with a toddler or pram will often be standing here, waiting to cross.

Basically this is a positioning fault and the nature of the road and buildings should alert a driver to the fact that extra care is needed on left turns. Why? Well try this for a bit of obscure information. The newer the road and buildings, the more gently curved are the street corners. Conversely, roads built 100 years ago in Victorian times, and as late as the 1920s, were constructed with sharp right angles for corners, as in Figure 2. Street corners can be graduated between the extremes of really sharp right angles and quite long, gentle curves, according to age. Not a lot of people know that, and its a real conversation stopper at a party.

Strangely, most Department for Transport publications, including *The Highway Code*, still illustrate these sharp right angled street corners. Heaven knows why – roads have not been built like this for 70 years or more.

Older roads often tend to be narrower roads, and on being instructed to turn left at such a corner, a learner might notice the sharp corner, and because of this and the restricted width of the road, he will tend to start steering round the corner before actually reaching it. A bit of pre-steering, so to speak. At first sight this might seem to be a sensible move, but in fact it's the worst thing one can do. Why? Because all this achieves is to move the car closer to the left hand kerb as the turning point approaches, and this is absolutely **not** the correct position in which to be.

Just turn back to those last two diagrams and look again at Figure 2. The hapless character with the rear wheels riding over the kerb, or the policeman's toes, is doing this because the vehicle was too close to the kerb on the approach to the point of turn.

All this is down to **observation**. In town driving particularly, you must be aware of every feature of the road and your surroundings. Is the road wet or slippery? Are there pedestrians, cyclists, dogs, prams, pregnant ladies, ice cream vans, kids, bus stops, concealed turnings, kamikaze skateboarders, pedestrian crossings, parked vehicles, wheeliebins, refuges with bollards in the centre of the road etc. etc. etc?

On top of all this, note the nature of the road itself, and this includes its age, which in turn will give you a strong clue as to the nature of the street corners. And that, my friends, is a strong clue to your positioning at left corners.

A final aspect of this positioning deals not with how far to the left or the right you should be, but how far forwards or back.

Consider the situation in which you are approaching a T junction or a crossroads where you are emerging from a minor road onto a major road. You are going to pause at the give way' line and assess the situation. Not every driver – learner or otherwise – has mastered the art of controlling the braking so that the vehicle stops smoothly, just at the give way line.

Stopping short, i.e. too soon, or overshooting, both constitute a positioning fault and also a braking fault. Stopping short means that you probably cannot see sufficiently far up or down the main road – if you can see at all. It's not all that serious however. You are, or should be, already in first gear so it's just a matter of bringing your clutch up a little above biting point and creeping gently up to the 'give way' line.

Overshooting is more serious. If you come to rest with part of your vehicle sticking out into the main road, you will certainly earn a major fault.

Have you noticed how so many easy-to-commit driving faults seem to automatically contravene more than one section of the examiner's marking sheet? Overshooting a 'give way' line is obviously a form of positioning fault, and we have looked at it in this section, which considers the subject of positioning.

It is also an obvious braking fault, (section 3). The driver has failed to plan the braking sufficiently early.

A fault also occurs under the first part of section 11, which deals with traffic signs and road markings – in this case the 'give way' sign, if any, and the 'give way' line on the road.

On top of these, failing to stop in time in this situation leaves the driver open to a charge of emerging without effective observation (section 15). Apart from earning the grave displeasure of the examiner in its many forms, overshooting puts you in risk of having the front of your car rearranged by a passing council sludgegulper.

I am often asked by pupils how one deals with the junctions where, having dutifully stopped at the 'give way' line one can still see absolutely nothing up or down the major road, let alone while actually approaching. Older roads which we discussed earlier, often have narrower footpaths and so buildings, hedges, fences etc. completely block the view, even though the vehicle is correctly stopped at the 'give way' line.

The procedure here is quite clear (unlike the visibility) You must first stop **at** the line – that's important. You then creep **slowly** (careful clutch control) until you reach a point where you have a clear view to both left and right. This might well involve looking through the windscreens and rear windows of cars parked on the main road. Creep and peep, creep and peep; taking careful account of larger vehicles approaching on the main road, particularly from your right.

You may well have to shuffle out quite a way before you have a clear view, and this calls for very careful footwork with your clutch and brake.

Make no mistake though, if you commit yourself to a full-blooded 'go' before you have a clear line of sight in both directions, then you are emerging without effective observation. This is a very common reason for test failure, it is particularly dangerous and is also a frequent cause of urban traffic accidents.

The whole subject of positioning at junctions, indeed at any hazard, is a long-winded business and we have discussed it at some length. Remember – Mirror, Signal Position, Speed and Gear.

We have been dealing here with **position** and **speed**. Remember, too, that we need to be **in the right place on the road at the right time**, at the **right speed** and in the **right gear**.

If you tackle any junction or hazard from the wrong place on the road or at the wrong speed, you will most likely end up in the wrong place on the road after your manoeuvre. All this simply emphasises the need to look ahead and plan ahead. In other words, **anticipate**.

Cutting right hand corners.

Of the four parts to section 15, relating to junctions, this is probably the easiest one to deal with. We know what is meant by not cutting right hand corners, it is illustrated here in Figure 1. You do not allow any part of your vehicle into the shaded area in the diagram.

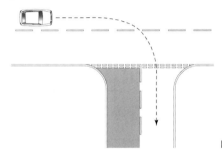

Figure 1   Driver A

I find that most learners become aware quite early that cutting right hand corners is one of the Deadly Sins. Unfortunately, many go to extreme lengths to avoid doing it, often with uncomfortable results. Look at Figure 2 – does it ring a bell?

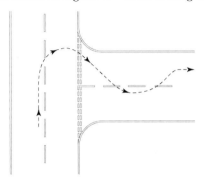

Figure 2   Driver B

Most beginners have fallen into this little trap and it involves badly 'oversteering' as you try to straighten up. It is the extreme opposite of cutting the corner. Cutting the corner is illustrated in Figure 3.

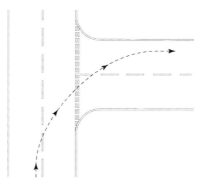

Figure 3   Driver C

It boils down to the fact that both drivers in Figures 2 and 3 started to steer the corner at the wrong time and the wrong place. Driver B turned too late, driver C too soon. In other words they started their turns at the wrong position in the road and so the question of cutting or not cutting right hand corners is really an extension of the previous subsection in which we discussed positioning the car correctly for right (or left) turns.

Having seen diagrams of turning too late and too soon, let's look at a driver who is getting it right, driver A. His actions are a half way compromise between the two we have already seen, a compromise between turning too soon and cutting the corner, and turning too late, which of course means having to turn far more steering wheel than is normally necessary and this results in finishing up on the wrong side of the road because the driver cannot straighten up in time (Look at Figure 2 again).

OK, so you turn too soon, cut the corner and earn a rap on the knuckles, or you turn too late, oversteer and have egg on your face. This next diagram shows how to get it right.

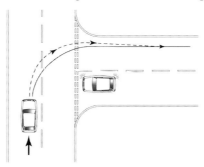

Figure 4   Driver D

As you can see this driver has steered a course which is a compromise between the previous two incorrect courses, and it's really quite simple. The driver has started to turn his steering wheel when about halfway along the 'give way' line. He has aimed so that his front offside (right hand) wheel misses the apex of the right angle formed by the 'give way' line and the hazard lines which lead up to it. (A 'give way' line is always preceded by about five hazard lines down the centre of the road). The diagram makes this clear.

This positioning will place the vehicle neatly in the correct place on the side road, following the turn. If there is a vehicle waiting to emerge from the side road and make a right turn (Figure 4), then this vehicle will be clearly visible to driver D who is approaching and turning into the side road. In such a case he would simply turn a little later, which in fact means a slightly sharper turn, and he would therefore make his turn a little more slowly. This modified course, necessitated by the waiting vehicle, is shown in the diagram by a dotted line.

Now a rather important. point comes up just here. This diagram we've been looking at, showing the correct path on a right turn, will appear rather different from many of the illustrations to be found in various learner driver publications. So many of these, including Department for Transport publications, illustrate vehicles executing a right turn as in Figure 5.

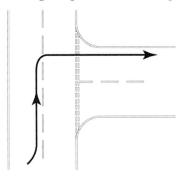

Figure 5

'Right', you may say, 'what's wrong with that'? Look again. Figure 5 depicts the path followed by a vehicle on which the steering wheel is **not** turned **until** after the vehicle has passed the centre of the road into which it is turning. It then appears to turn right through 90 degrees, virtually within its own length.

Now if this manoeuvre were attempted for real, what happened next would depend on the width of the side road and whether the corner was a gentle curve or one of these sharp right angle jobs. At best our unfortunate driver would hopelessly oversteer, and at worst he would end up in the front garden of the gent who lived in the corner house.

Let's draw the diagram again, but with one small addition (Figure 6).

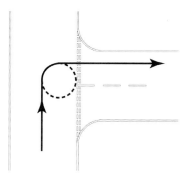

Figure 6

The car turns through 90 degrees, around the circumference of a very small circle. We have continued round the rest of the same circle with a dotted line through the remainder of the 360 degrees. We finish up with the impression of a vehicle which can turn a complete circle in an area less than half the width of the road. (Useful for parking?) Even a London taxi can't do this, and it's worth noting that the diameter of the turning circle of the average car is in excess of 10 metres (30 feet).

The point I'm making here is that a normal car cannot turn a corner as shown in Figure 5, even though some illustrations suggest it. In real life you have to follow a curved path, as shown in Figures 1 and 4. So don't be misled by illustrations like Figure 5.

In this final part of our look at section 15 of the test we're dealing with *'cutting'*, or not cutting, *'right hand corners'*. We have seen that the subject is inevitably tied in with the previous sub-section, *'positioning'*. It's not too late therefore to offer a final thought on turning right, in which the key factor is again positioning. The diagram on the following page illustrates the situation.

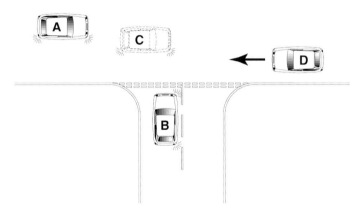

Car A is waiting to turn right into a side road, and he has to stop to give way to oncoming traffic car D. Car B is waiting in the side road to emerge into the main road, turning right. Where exactly should car A wait?

The diagram shows that he has in fact stopped too soon. Why is his position wrong? Well, as soon as car D (oncoming traffic) has passed, it will be safe for A to turn into the side road, but B may think it is now safe to emerge and make his right turn **because A has stopped so far short of the turning**.

He is wrong of course. He can see A's right indicator and should realise that A has priority, but because A has positioned himself so badly, B is quite likely to seize the opportunity and nip out under A's nose.

A is guilty of bad positioning and if he presents B with the opportunity to go first he is also guilty of '*undue hesitation*'.

In this situation A should have gone further forward and stopped about halfway along the 'give way' line at the point where he would start to steer the turn (position C).

A word of warning. When you find yourself in A's situation – but hopefully at position C – don't start to turn the steering wheel before you actually stop. Why not? Well, if you receive a bash up the rear end from a following vehicle – and it does happen – then, with your front wheels turned to the right, you will be pushed across to the right into the path of an oncoming vehicle. Just a small but worthwhile precaution.

This section on the important subject of junctions, with its four sub-sections, gives considerable scope for major faults. Many tests are failed under one of these headings. Certainly the old adage of being in the right place on the road at the right time, at the right speed for the task and in the right gear for the speed, is never more valid than at road junctions.

To back a winning horse you can't do better than a tip from the stables, so with acknowledgements to the Driving Instructors Association magazine, *Driving*, I offer you the following quote from the Examiners' Training Manual.

There you are then, the whole of section 15 in one paragraph.

'When turning left or right at junctions the candidate should be advised well before coming to the junction. The examiner should observe whether the candidate brings the vehicle under proper control, takes due account of the type of junction and any warning signs, takes rear observation, gives the proper signals in good time, takes up the proper position before turning, adjusts speed, gives him/ herself a good line of vision before emerging and at once adopts the proper position in the new road after turning'

SECTION 16 OF THE TEST

Overtaking, meeting and crossing the path of other vehicles

Once again, one section in the test but several aspects to consider.

Overtaking

Do you remember the first time you overtook another vehicle? It may only have been a farm tractor, but it was a memorable milestone in your motoring life. Overtaking means passing another road user going in the same direction as yourself, i.e. something moving. You don't 'overtake' a stationary vehicle, you only 'pass' it.

Often there is no occasion to overtake on the test, except perhaps bicycles. However if your test route takes you out of a town centre onto roads with higher speed limits and you catch up with a slower moving vehicle, the examiner will expect you to overtake when it is safe and prudent to do so. Taking the line of least resistance and pottering along behind the slower vehicle, would certainly earn you a 'fail' under Section 14 of the test, failing to *'make progress'*.

Overtaking needs some accurate and complex assessments. Apart from the width and length (length is most important) of the vehicle you wish to overtake, you need to assess its speed – assuming that it is not actually accelerating. Next you need to know your speed in relation to his, and to what speed you can reasonably expect to accelerate in order to overtake quickly. The greater the difference between his speed and yours, the sooner you can get past him and return to the correct side of the road.

If you can only manage a speed of 10 mph faster than his, it will take at least 10 seconds to perform the task, and if you are doing, say, 40 mph then you will travel some 600 metres on the wrong side of the road while doing so. Moreover, the longer the overtaken vehicle, the greater the time needed for the manoeuvre.

The two principal errors in overtaking are (1) not seizing the opportunity to overtake when it occurs, and (2) failing to build up enough speed to do the job quickly, and this indicates a lack of confidence. Obviously the faster you travel the sooner you finish the task and return to your own side of the road.

Part of failing to build up speed lies in not dropping down to a lower gear before starting the manoeuvre. Dropping down a gear will depend on your speed at the time, but usually you have reduced speed on catching up the slower vehicle while you check that the road ahead is clear.

At this point, if you change down from 5th to 4th, or at a lower speed (or in a 4 speed gearbox car) from 4th to 3rd, you will get much greater acceleration in the lower gear.

It does sound odd, I know, to change down in order to go faster. This goes against the basic teaching you received on the use of gears. It is a fact, however, that although a lower gear will not produce such a high top speed, it will give you more power and sharper acceleration. If you find this difficult to accept, ask your instructor to give you a demonstration, and a chat on the principles of overtaking, with particular reference to rapid acceleration.

Another common fault when overtaking is coming too close to the vehicle in front before looking beyond it to see if the road is clear ahead. Look at these two diagrams.

 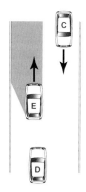

Figure 1   **Figue 2**

In Figure 1 driver A cannot see vehicle C approaching. If he pulls out now for a look, he stands a good chance of a head-on collision and this exact scenario is the basis of many serious and horrific accidents.

In Figure 2, driver D has held back from vehicle E and by moving only slightly to the right, he has a good clear view of the road ahead. In the event of oncoming traffic, he has room enough to move back to the left, remaining at a safe distance behind E. Driver A however has left himself no room to get back in behind B, on catching sight of C.

So, hang back, check mirrors carefully; (a vehicle behind might be about to overtake **you**). Move out to the right for a look. If the road ahead is clear for a sufficient distance, and you are sure that you can comfortably travel faster than the chap in front, then go, and the faster the better. Don't forget to signal. If the driver you are overtaking is using his mirrors, he then knows exactly what you intend to do.

So far we have looked at a manoeuvre in which just two vehicles are involved, yours and the one you plan to overtake. This is fairly simple, but now let's introduce a third vehicle.

Assume that when you go out for a look you see another vehicle coming towards you. Now what? Well taking a rather extreme case, if this third vehicle is a mile away, and travelling at walking speed, you obviously have plenty of time to overtake the vehicle in front of you. The nearer this third vehicle is and the faster it is travelling, the nearer you get to the point where you cannot **safely** overtake and return to your own side of the road in good time.

You can see from all this that your first thought on seeing the oncoming vehicle must be 'how far away is it, and how fast is it travelling?'

If your estimate of these factors points to your still going on with your original plan, i.e. to overtake the vehicle in front, then you must be quite certain that you can do this without either cutting in sharply in front of the overtaken vehicle, or causing any danger, inconvenience or anxiety to the oncoming driver.

Consider the fact that if you overtake at 40 mph, and the oncoming vehicle is travelling at 60 mph, you jointly have a combined or 'closing' speed of 100 mph. This in turn means that the gap between you is decreasing at the rate of **50 metres every second**. You can see therefore, that to overtake safely when there is an oncoming vehicle, that vehicle needs to be a healthy distance away and not travelling excessively fast.

Let us just recap on what is involved in this type of situation.

There are several important factors. There is your speed and the speed to which you can accelerate; there is the speed of the vehicle you wish to overtake and its length; there is the distance away of the oncoming vehicle, and finally its speed. Knowing these factors, the sums would be easy if only you had a computer, but you haven't. You have only the brain you were born with, and that works largely on experience.

I'm sure by now you will have realised that it takes a very skilled and experienced driver to take in all these factors at a glance, and immediately say 'yes we go' or 'no it's not on'.

We spoke earlier of the golden rule at junctions i.e. **if in doubt, don't**. Nowhere is that advice more appropriate than when considering whether or not to overtake.

I left out one further aspect of the overtaking task, when we were talking about going out for a look. Not only are we looking ahead to see if the road is clear of oncoming traffic, we are looking at the features of the road itself. Is there a bend in the road or a dip which prevents you seeing as far ahead as you need to see? Are there road markings which prevent you from crossing beyond the centre? Are there traffic signs or road markings that indicate that overtaking is prohibited, or that you are approaching a hazard, such as a junction?

Wrongly tackled, overtaking can be a most dangerous manoeuvre, but don't imagine you can 'get by' by just never doing it. You must become familiar with the task, and there is no substitute for practice. In my experience too many learners are short of both instruction and practice in this important area. Your instructor should find simple overtaking situations for you whenever possible. Practise these and you will gain both experience and confidence.

We saw that adding an oncoming vehicle to an overtaking situation brought a new and more hazardous aspect to the task. It also leads us neatly into the second section of this chapter, which deals with meeting other vehicles safely.

Meeting other vehicles (safely)

This is by no means an uncommon cause of test failure. It results from a failure to look far enough ahead and anticipate what effect an oncoming vehicle will have on your plans, and also a failure to be accurately aware of the width of both your vehicle and the oncoming one.

You are by now well aware that if there is an obstruction, moving or stationary, on your side of the road then you must not move out to pass it if this will result in any danger or inconvenience to any oncoming road user. In other words you give way and let the oncoming vehicle come through first, unless the road is wide enough for you to pass the obstruction and still leave enough room for the oncoming vehicle. (We must also consider this situation in the light of section 18 of the test, which requires you to leave adequate space for stationary vehicles.)

Now, assume the situation is reversed, and the obstruction is on the other side of the road. Oncoming traffic should now hold back and let you through, but will they? Alas, not always. A large vehicle such as a bus or a rampant bin-wagon in full cry is more difficult to stop and restart than your car, and frequently such a vehicle will pull out to pass its obstruction and intimidate you into giving way.

It should be understood that when piloting a large vehicle, one's approach to traffic problems is a little different to that of the District Nurse in her Nissan Micra. My experience of driving bin wagons is, alas, somewhat limited, but I have driven some pretty big vehicles, and one tends to get a different perspective on the problems. You don't expect cars to tangle with you, and as a rule they don't. It would be a uniquely courteous trucker who brought his big artic, with 30 tons of tree-trunks aboard, to a grinding halt so that you can sail through in your Mini. I know the good book says that that's what should happen, but don't count on it.

In circumstances such as these therefore, it's no good you saying 'well it's my priority so I'm going through' when it is patently obvious that the approaching juggernaut has no intention of giving way. You have failed to anticipate the actions of the opposition, and the examiner here would fault you for failing to '*meet other vehicles safely*'. That is unless he has already leapt out of the car, which might prove to be a very prudent move. The oncoming driver is guilty, admittedly, of a lack of manners but you are equally guilty of a lack of common sense, and you would fail.

The Queen's Highway has sadly developed into an arena, or battlefield, where contests are fought daily. Do not expect either on your test or under any other driving circumstances that other road users can be relied upon to act either correctly or even sensibly. Poor driving by others will often put you in a position where you will have to take action in order to 'meet vehicles safely'.

Consider this illustration.

We have a hazard similar to this quite close to our local test centre. Vehicle A comes round a left hand bend and immediately encounters parked vehicles on both sides of the road. The remaining gap leaves barely enough space for two cars to pass. In the event of a lorry coming through, there is not enough room for any other vehicle, and lorries here are frequent. There is no clear case of a priority since there are obstructions on both sides of the road.

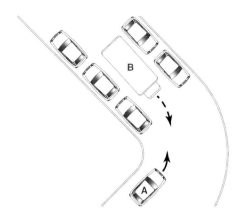

In our illustration vehicle B is committed to coming through the bottleneck before he is visible to vehicle A. Vehicle A must naturally stop and let B come through.

Countless times test candidates have found themselves in vehicle A's situation, and have failed their test through not assessing the situation correctly. They have attempted to enter the bottle-neck, only to find they have had to stop and reverse in order to let the opposing vehicle come through. This seems to happen far too often and it is a good example of a lack of both good manners, common sense and forward planning.

It is most important that you learn to assess your vehicle's width, remembering that when you are in the driving seat, you have more car to your left than to your right.

Ideally, to pass an oncoming vehicle safely, you need a gap of about an open door's width between you and the approaching vehicle and also between you and a vehicle parked on your left. It is obviously no use concentrating on leaving a good clear gap between you and the oncoming vehicle while at the same time systematically ripping the driver's door off the car parked on your left.

Whether we consider a gap between you and a parked vehicle on your left, or between you and an oncoming vehicle, you must reduce speed if the gap is less than an open door's width. The smaller the gap the more slowly you go. If you are in any doubt as to the width of gap you will have when your two vehicles are alongside each other, then stop altogether and let the oncoming vehicle come through first. We are obviously talking here about a fairly narrow street, so if you have to stop you must choose a sensible place, for example between two parked vehicles if possible, so as to minimise the obstruction to the oncoming vehicle.

Don't overdo it however. It is all too easy to teach caution and courtesy to a pupil and finish up with a driver who comes to a standstill on every possible occasion. If you stop every time you encounter a vehicle coming towards you, you will surely fail under section 14 of the test, ('undue hesitation'). This is why it is so important for you to become accurately and confidently familiar with the actual size of your vehicle so that you can immediately recognise the size of gaps you can safely go through and, of course, the ones you can't.

Crossing the path of other vehicles (safely)

This is perhaps the easiest of these three sub-sections. When you cross the path of another vehicle you are almost invariably turning to the right, and there is one golden rule which applies when you do this. It is in fact the legend that was carved upon The Great Tablet, countless years ago.

Indeed, had Moses been able to look ahead, beyond the days of mule-drawn traffic, this might well have been the eleventh commandment.

It only applies of course in countries where traffic drives on the left, as we do. Because we drive on the left we inevitably cross the path of oncoming traffic if we turn to the right. We made the point earlier that turning to the right is always more hazardous than turning left, and it is because we have to cross the path of other vehicles that this is so.

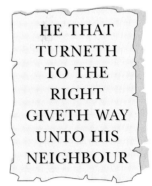

HE THAT TURNETH TO THE RIGHT GIVETH WAY UNTO HIS NEIGHBOUR

I have always taught my pupils this vital commandment, '**he that turneth to the right giveth way unto his neighbour**'. The biblical phraseology always causes a smile, and helps it to stick in the memory. It **must** stick in the memory since it governs virtually all conduct at road junctions.

Road junctions constitute a very important subject, as we have seen, and it is odd that such a very complex subject should be governed by comparatively few rules. The majority of these are contained in section 15 of the test, in relation to road junctions. The final rule is this 'eleventh commandment'. It is simple but absolutely vital.

There are inevitably local exceptions to any procedure, but at any hazard, if for some reason our rule did not apply, then the alternative procedure would be clearly signed, either by road markings or traffic signs.

What is meant by crossing another vehicle's path safely? Well, you apply exactly the same set of standards as you applied when you emerged from a side road.

You ask yourself the four-part question; if I pull out in front of this approaching car, will he have to alter course, or slow down? Will he be put to any danger or inconvenience?

This same yardstick is applied to turning right across the path of an oncoming vehicle. If you cause him to take any sort of avoiding action, or cause any inconvenience, you commit a serious and probably dangerous driving error and it is obviously a major test fault.

On this question of turning to the right, here is a small problem that often puzzles pupils in the early stages. Look at this diagram.

Car A wants to turn to the right into the side road. Car B is going straight down the main road. Car C is waiting to emerge from the side road, and turn to the right. Who has priority?

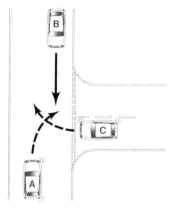

Clearly; car A gives way to car B, because car A is turning right. Now, when car B has passed by and gone, car A is still waiting to turn right. Does he give way to car C? No he does not.

Car C is also turning right, as it happens, but the situation now has nothing to do with anyone turning right. The situation is now governed by the fact that car A is on a main road, while car C is emerging from a side road, and must act on the 'give way' signs. Therefore car A goes next.

Read through that again if it is not absolutely clear. A gives way to B, then A makes his right turn, and finally C goes, having acted on the 'give way' signs.

Now, let's consider another aspect of turning right, with its possibility of crossing the path of oncoming traffic.

Learners and indeed many experienced drivers are frequently unsure about how to turn to the right when an oncoming or opposing vehicle is also wishing to turn to his right. Do they pass nearside to nearside, or offside to offside, and what on earth do these expressions mean anyway? See Figures 1 and 2 on the following page.

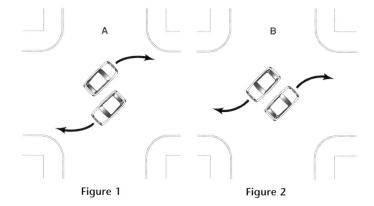

Figure 1   Figure 2

Figure 1 shows two cars, each turning right at a crossroads. They are passing each other with the offside (right hand side) of one car next to the offside of the other.

Figure 2 shows the cars passing with their nearsides (left hand sides) close to each other.

The Highway Code advises in rule number 157, that when opposing vehicles are both turning to the right they should pass offside to offside, as in diagram A. In my experience, and as a very rough and general guide only, the offside to offside rule tends to be commonly practised in London, and some larger cities. In provincial towns however, the accepted practice seems to be to pass nearside to nearside, as in Figure 2. In fact in many towns, busy crossroads with traffic lights have arrows painted on the road, in the centre of the junction, which indicate that vehicles turning to the right SHOULD pass nearside to nearside with opposing traffic which is also making a right turn..

Both methods have their advantages and disadvantages, and can be the subject of lengthy debates on 'roadcraft'.

Bearing in mind that our purpose is to ensure that we get it right on our test what should you, the learner, do in this situation? The answer is simple. Take your cue from the car coming towards you. If you are approaching a crossroads with instructions to turn to the right, and you have an oncoming vehicle which is signalling his intention to also turn right, (his right, not yours), then let him position himself for the turn, and go along with his plan. See Figure 3 on the following page.

In Figure 3, you are in car B, about to turn right. Car A is approaching you and signalling a right turn. If this gent starts his turn when he reaches point X, then he obviously intends to cut across in front of you, and pass nearside to nearside, following the path of the dotted line.

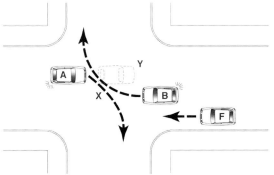

Figure 3

Now faced with this clear intention of his, it would be a bit daft for you to insist on the rule 157 preferred method. That would mean you moving further forward in order to keep to the left of him, intending to go round his rear end. Since he has already started his right turn, he would finish up coming into your car via the driver's door. (You would fail for this under section 21 of the test, *'anticipation of the actions of other road users'*).

No, the answer here is to follow his lead, make your own right turn, following the dotted line shown leading round to the right **in front** of car B. On the other hand, if he comes straight forward to point Y on the diagram, then you would follow his lead and carry on forward until you could pass round the back of him, thus passing offside to offside, as the good book suggests.

You may, however, be unable to avoid arriving at the critical turning point slightly before he does. In this case it would certainly be better to do as *The Highway Code* rule 157 suggests, and position yourself for turning offside to offside, and hope the other gent has the good sense to follow your lead.

If there are arrows marked on the road which indicate how you should turn right, then you do, of course, follow the arrows.

It is difficult to lay down hard and fast guidelines on his subject. Many factors can influence the way the two cars make their turn. The width of the road, the actual layout of the crossroads and various other factors, including road markings, can decide how the two drivers react.

We do have a large crossroads junction locally, where arrows painted on the road actually tell drivers to pass near-side to nearside. A candidate who failed to comply with the arrows would not be marked for a 'positioning' fault, but for failing to '*take appropriate action on all road markings*' (section 11a).

Look at the last diagram again. The two cars A and B would seem to have nothing to prevent them from safely making their right turns, but now let's introduce car F to the scene. F is coming up behind B intending, quite correctly, to overtake it on its left hand side, since B has given a right signal and positioned itself toward the centre of the road prior to turning. Now the driver of car A cannot see car F because it is hidden from view by car B. Similarly any vehicle overtaking car A on its left side would be invisible to car B.

This is the principal argument against turning nearside to nearside, and many a careless and avoidable accident occurs under just these circumstances. Remember, he that turneth to the right giveth way unto his neighbour, and that includes giving way to he that lurketh, unseen, behind another vehicle.

To sum up, if the decision is clearly yours, go for the offside to offside turn, as the good book suggests. Don't be surprised however, if the other driver opts for the short cut and turns right in front of you. In this case you must hastily change to plan B, and go along with the opposition. If you don't, you risk a collision.

Don't ever be ashamed to change your mind. There is a great deal of mind-changing in driving, since other factors and circumstances can change so rapidly. It is not a sign of weakness to change your plan, it's a sure sign that you are 'on the ball'.

Failure to be flexible and capable of revising your plan at short notice can earn you a major fault under the last section but one of the test, section 21. This is probably the most wide ranging but least detailed of them all, and it requires you to '*show awareness and anticipation of the actions of other road users*'. We'll come to that later.

SECTION 17 OF THE TEST

Positioning the vehicle and lane discipline

Position of the vehicle during normal driving

When test failure results from a fault in positioning the vehicle it's usually down to either inattention, forgetfulness or not confidently knowing the width of the vehicle, and therefore the position of the front nearside wheel.

On a quiet road with few hazards it is easy to be concentrating on mirror, hands in the correct position on the wheel, foot not resting on the clutch pedal, and so on, so you completely forget to notice whereabouts you are on the road.

Often, on a quiet housing estate with little traffic about, I have to say to a pupil, 'Lift off the gas pedal, I'm going to stop you', and with the dual controls I stop the car.

The pupil looks at me accusingly and says 'Why have we stopped here?'

My reply is 'Well, if there were a white line down the centre of the road, whereabouts would it be in relation to the car?'

Had there been a white line, and there often isn't on minor roads, it would have passed right underneath the centre of the car. Then the penny drops.

The rough and ready guideline here is 'Don't drive in the gutter, but don't drive in the middle of the road'. As with many other correct driving procedures, this positioning thing eventually becomes instinctive, but until it does you must constantly monitor your correct position on the road.

In the absence of parked vehicles, oncoming vehicles or other hazards, your position on the open road for normal driving should be about an open door's width, or about a metre from the left side of the road.

Remember, we said that we should leave a metre gap when passing stationary vehicles. This metre from the kerb and from stationary obstructions is known as 'following the safety line'.

A number of factors will affect your position; the width of the road, parked vehicles and cyclists. In fact any hazard will influence your position – remember Mirror, Signal, **Position**, Speed and Gear.

Another factor which influences the position on the road, and is often missed by beginners, concerns oncoming vehicles. I often find, when teaching on a wide main road, that we have oncoming vehicles, one of which is overtaking another, so we have two approaching vehicles side-by-side. The road may well be wide enough for this to be done quite safely, but only if we are prepared to ease into the left a little. The sight of the two oncoming juggernauts ought, as Dr. Johnson said, to concentrate the mind wonderfully.

Unfortunately a learner often fails to react to this stimulus, and ploughs happily on down the centre of the road, despite the fact that we have three or four metres of unused road on our left.

We have three faults here, positioning, failure to 'meet other vehicles safely' and also failure to 'be aware of and anticipate the actions of other road users'.

I sometimes wonder if the learner fondly imagines that the oncoming driver is going to pull back on his steering wheel and fly over us, 'Thunderbird' fashion.

At this point I usually have to suggest that we move to the left a bit in order to give the oncoming chap a bit of elbow room, since the distance between us is diminishing at the rate of about 50 metres every second.

Another important aspect of positioning, often overlooked, is your position when being overtaken.

You should of course always know when you are about to be overtaken. How do you know? Mirror. Mirror, mirror, and still more mirror. All the time.

Every 10 or 12 seconds have a quick glance to the rear. There are few things more alarming than catching your first glimpse of a whacking great overtaking long-distance coach when he is right alongside you, just outside your door.

Never be caught like this. MIRROR.

If a faster vehicle wishes to overtake you, it is polite and prudent to move a little to your left if there is room to do so, particularly if

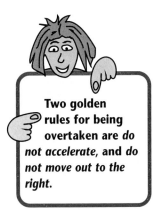

Two golden rules for being overtaken are *do not accelerate*, and *do not move out to the right*.

it is a large vehicle. Note that you do not need to slow down. The overtaking driver should have based his plan on your present speed, and he will assume that you will maintain it.

This baulking of overtaking vehicles inevitably conjures up thoughts of an infamous group of motorway drivers who are all paid-up members of C L 0 C, (the Centre Lane Owners Club). The principal pastime of this group is to potter along in the centre lane while the left hand lane remains empty. The large goods vehicle and the towed caravan, which are not allowed in the right hand lane, are therefore prevented from overtaking and remain stuck behind these selfish, ill mannered idiots.

Your theory test may well question you on the subject of motorway positioning, and correct lane discipline. Its in *The Highway Code*.

Just look it up again in *The Highway Code*. Go on, do it now. We'll wait for you. (It's rule 238).

We know that positioning for normal driving usually means being about a metre (three feet) or an open door's width from the left hand kerb. On urban roads and country lanes this would usually mean having the offside (the right hand side) of the car about the same distance from the centre line of the road. If there is no centre line, you must imagine one. All this, of course, assumes that you are taking account of parked cars, cyclists, children larking about near the edge of the pavement, and so on.

Figure 1 shows your position on this sort of road.

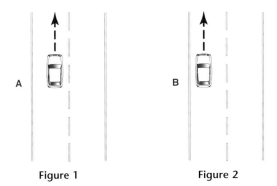

A   B

Figure 1   **Figure 2**

On a wider, more main road, your metre from the kerb will place you nearer to the kerb than to the centre of the road. Figure 2 shows this position. On such roads, you will find that if you mentally divide your half of the road into three parts, then you will be about one third out from the left hand edge, and two thirds in from the centre.

We have said already that it's not always easy to know the exact position of the nearside edge of your car, since you are sitting in the right hand seat.

A great help here is a quick look in the nearside door or wing mirror. If this is correctly adjusted, you should see both the nearside of your car and the nearside kerb.

Driving with this metre gap on the left is known as following a 'safety line', and the gap should be kept at this level when steering round parked vehicles and similar obstructions. Remember – mirror before moving out for the obstruction, and of course, the sooner you begin to move out, the less steering wheel you will need to turn. Elementary geometry.

On any multi-lane road, dual or single carriageway, always stay in the nearside lane, except when overtaking or approaching a junction or roundabout where you intend to turn right. Stay also within the lanes marked by the lane lines on the road, just as you would observe the lane line markings at a junction.

Remember again our aim of being in the right place on the road at the right time. Default on this and you risk test failure, and probably actual danger.

At all times, your position in the road is dictated, as are virtually all your decisions, by good manners and common sense. It is achieved by having had a good grounding in basic vehicle handling during your early lessons, with particular emphasis on knowing exactly whereabouts on the road both sides of your vehicle are at any time.

Exercise lane discipline

Lane discipline means several different things. It applies particu-larly where your half of the road is marked out into lanes by broken white lines painted on the road. This occurs at junctions on main roads, at roundabouts and at many other features where there is a choice of routes ahead. These lanes are often marked with arrows which are designed to get vehicles into the correct position in the road, depending on which route they intend to take a little further on.

In section 15 of the test, dealing with positioning the vehicle correctly for junctions, the point was made that you should decide which lane you need to be in, get into it and stay in it. Don't then drift or wander sideways so that part of your vehicle is in one lane, part in the adjacent lane.

That is lane discipline in a nutshell, although there is a little more to it than that.

Here are three different examples of typical lane markings which might be found on the approach to a junction.

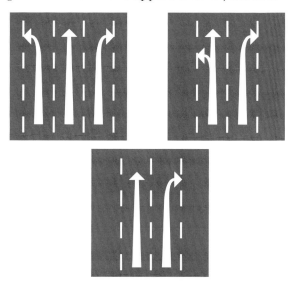

You will see that the lane for following the road straight ahead is usually the left lane. Sometime it's the right hand lane, often it can be both.

A word of caution on this. If you approach a junction where there is a right turn available and **both** lanes are marked for 'straight ahead' and you are, in fact, going straight ahead, then take the **left** lane. Leave the right hand lane for traffic intending to turn to the right.

How often one sees the following scenario. Large junction with crossroads. Traffic lights. Both lanes shown available for straight ahead. Traffic lights at 'red'. Vehicles in both lanes, no vehicle showing a right indicator. Lights turn green – both lanes move forward. The front car in the right hand lane moves out to the centre of the junction, stops and only then puts on a right indicator. He waits, giving way to oncoming traffic before making his right turn, and a whole string of vehicles who were expecting to move straight ahead are stuck behind this mindless wally, simply because he did not have the good manners and common sense to indicate 'right' as he approached the junction.

A signal should tell others what you propose to do, not what you're halfway through doing.

This sort of appalling stupidity is all too common, and for this reason the examiner will expect. you to take the left lane for straight ahead, if both lanes are marked as available for straight ahead.

I said earlier that there was more to lane discipline than being correctly within the marked confines of the lane. There are many places where, in a busy town with heavy traffic, the road is wide enough to take two moving lines of traffic side-by-side, although they are not separated by a marked lane line.

Choose your lane in the light of where you are going further down the road. A left turn? A right turn? If, as far as you know, you will stay on the same road, then choose the left lane, for the reason spelled out above.

The important thing is to stay in your chosen lane, don't wander about so that you are half in one lane, half in the other. If you must change lanes, do so with proper observation, signalling clearly and in good time.

This book is about passing your test, and motorways play no part in the driving test. A comment on motorways, however, is very relevant when discussing lane discipline. You will discover, once you have passed your test and actually use motorways, that lane discipline on British motorways leaves a lot to be desired. Both the Americans and the Germans put us to shame in this respect.

Enough of this for now except to urge you to read the motorway section of *The Highway Code* thoroughly. Learn what is said about lane discipline and let it really sink in. You will need it later, and it will certainly crop up in the theory test.

As you can see, lane discipline is closely linked to positioning for normal driving and also to the earlier section on positioning for junctions.

SECTION 18 OF THE TEST

Passing stationary vehicles

This section follows naturally after the previous one, since if you don't allow adequate clearance for any obstruction, you are not positioning the vehicle correctly. So shaving too closely past a parked vehicle is also a positioning fault, and if you think about it, it could be a steering fault as well.

Whether this is so really depends on why you were too close to the parked vehicle. If you pass it with only inches to spare deliberately, in other words you meant to pass so close, then it is a positioning fault, but if you had planned to leave adequate space but somehow got closer to it than you meant to, then that would be a steering fault.

You may remember that we have discussed the problem of getting the nearside back wheel over the kerb when turning a sharp left hand corner. In this situation also, the error could be either incorrect positioning or faulty steering.

Stationary vehicles are both a current and potential hazard. The parked car sitting there in the gutter is already a hazard because it will cause you to alter course. Maybe because of oncoming traffic you might also need to reduce speed, or even stop. As you come alongside it, however, it could produce further perils. One of its doors might be flung open, or a previously unseen child could run out from in front of it.

It is quite possible to kill a cyclist with the edge of a carelessly opened door. The same door, struck at a critical angle, could actually write off one or both cars.

Never open a car door, on either side, without first carefully checking for cycles, vehicles or pedestrians.

So we need this open door's width, or about a metre of clear space when passing stationary vehicles. Narrow streets and oncoming traffic may make this difficult to achieve however.

When discussing '*meeting vehicles safely*' we agreed there was no point in leaving a safe gap between you and the oncoming vehicle, if this meant tearing the door mirrors off the cars parked on our left. The converse of this is equally true. A safe metre from the parked cars and four centimetres between you and the oncoming vehicle is not the right answer either. So often the inexperienced driver fails to look at the overall gap through which he must pass. He looks only to one side, usually the right, since that is where the oncoming vehicle will approach. No thought is given to how much gap is being allowed on the left.

A more experienced and confident driver will look at the total width of the available gap, and put his vehicle right through the centre of it, leaving equal space on each side.

We have just discussed a situation in which there was a metre to spare on one side and only four centimetres on the other. This amounts to a gap of 104 centimetres. Divide that by two, and we should leave about half metre on each side, and that is exactly what the experienced driver would do.

Now a gap of about half metre is not a lot, and although it does not mean you need to actually stop, there certainly is a need to slow right down. A useful rough guide is that if you can leave about a metre gap on either side, then any speed up to 30 mph is reasonable.

Reduce this gap to two thirds of a metre and your speed would need to be no more than 20 mph, a second gear situation.

For a gap of one third of a metre or less, then we are talking about walking speed at the most, or a complete stop while you check and think.

Section 16 of the test on overtaking mentioned the need to know exactly where the sides of your vehicle are. Just now we spoke of confidently driving through a gap leaving one third of a metre on each side. Could you do just that? You should be able to if you are up to test standard.

Acquiring this judgement is something which can easily be practised at home. Failing this, your instructor will help you. One way is to find a quiet road and place a cardboard box in the road, about a car's width out from the kerb. Drive past it, getting closer each time, judging how much space you are leaving.

If you can find a deserted car park or a field, so much the better. Put out two boxes to represent the gap between you and an oncoming vehicle and drive through, leaving an equal gap on each side. As you progress, make the gaps smaller, and practise until you really know just where the extremities of your car are.

We've been discussing stationary vehicles, but section 18 of the test refers to stationary vehicles and **obstructions**. This is included to cater for car-sized hazards such as builders' or rubbish skips.

Failure to leave sufficient space for stationary vehicles betrays either poor judgement on the driver's part or a lack of awareness of the dangers involved. It is also alarming and uncomfortable for any passenger in the nearside front seat, and this of course is where the examiner sits.

Nothing prompts an instructor or an examiner to cover the dual controls, ready for immediate intervention, more than being driven too close to stationary vehicles.

Most learners tend to think their vehicle is larger than it really is, which is probably not a bad thing. Certainly better than thinking it's smaller than it really is. Early training and practice in this area will make for much more accurate and confident driving in traffic.

Demonstrate to the examiner that you are both confident and competent at handling your vehicle in confined spaces, and his confidence in you will be measured accordingly.

SECTION 19 OF THE TEST

Pedestrian crossings

This is not a section which claims a large number of failures, and those who do come unstuck usually do so through insufficient observation and/or poor anticipation.

To be able to take the correct action at pedestrian crossings, you must thoroughly know the legal requirements for drivers at the 4 main types of crossing. These are zebra, pelican, puffin and toucan crossings – all listed in the pedestrian section of *The Highway Code*, (sections 19, 22 and 25).

In addition, traffic lights at junctions often have a pedestrian crossing function as well, and have a crossing area marked by studs in the road, just forward of the vehicle stop line. Markings at both zebra and pelican crossings are clearly illustrated in the pedestrian crossings section of *The Driving Test*.

There is more to pedestrian crossings than you might think. I suggest you go carefully through *The Highway Code* again, checking everything to do with crossings, including the rules in the pedestrians' section.

Learn the requirements for drivers and pedestrians at each type of crossing. Learn what the various road markings mean, particularly the white zig-zags on the approach to a crossing.

Memorise the rule concerning not parking or overtaking in the area approaching a crossing, that is the area marked by the zig-zag white lines. Learn what the different types of pedestrian refuges in the centre of the road look like. With a refuge there, is it now two separate crossings, or still only one? Not quite as simple as it seems.

When a test is failed at a pedestrian crossing, then often the candidate has fallen into the common error of waving a hesitant pedestrian across the road. This of course is an incorrect signal and the failure would be marked under section 10 of the test, *'give signals correctly'*. We discussed this on page 79. We looked at how we might legally persuade our timid pedestrian to cross the road without actually waving them on, which would certainly incur a major fault as an incorrect signal.

Another cause of failure is inadvertently stopping, in a queue of traffic, with your car actually astride a pedestrian crossing, be it pelican or zebra. It results from lack of anticipation, not reading the road ahead, or realising that in this stop-go-stop situation, a pedestrian crossing is just ahead.

Stopping on the crossing like this results in the next clutch of pedestrians who cross having to either detour round the front or rear of your car, banging on the boot with umbrellas, and making rude suggestions as they go, or at the worst, scrambling over the top. (I have actually seen this done.)

Any pedestrian who has stepped onto a zebra crossing as you approach has priority.

If, at a zebra crossing, a pedestrian is standing by the kerb, obviously waiting to cross, you should stop for them, even though they have not actually started to cross.

Do note also, that the lady who pushes her pram onto the crossing, but who still has her feet on the footpath, **has legally started to cross**, and so again has priority.

If this lady, or any pedestrian, is the only person using the crossing, then you, the driver, do not need to wait until she has reached the opposite footpath. You may move on once this person has safely passed the front of your car, but you must not harass them by revving your engine or creeping forward as they pass in front of you.

Before moving on again you must always look both ways, to make sure there are no more pedestrians about to cross.

An observant driver will anticipate a pedestrian crossing from some distance away. Look at the footpaths on both sides of the road. Look for the potential crossers. Once you have decided that you must give way to a pedestrian, give the 'slowing down' arm signal if you have following traffic, and then all concerned, including the pedestrians, will be well aware of your intentions.

Do be aware of, and considerate to, the elderly, the infirm, the blind, or any handicapped person. We are all pedestrians at some time, and the driver/pedestrian relationship works much better when based on good manners and common sense on the part of all road users.

This was sadly not the case in a little cameo I witnessed a couple of weeks ago.

I was walking towards a zebra crossing when a young man pushed past me in a great hurry, and launched himself onto the crossing without a glance in either direction. This caused the driver of a Volvo to do a rapid emergency stop, narrowly missing the fleeing youth.

This driver, whose window was open, yelled some pertinent advice to the culprit, but I failed to hear the words since they were drowned by the noise of a closely following bread van walloping into the back of the Volvo.

The high-speed young pedestrian must have caught some hint of the Volvo driver's displeasure, for he paused in mid-flight, turned, and giving a definitely unofficial signal yelled, 'Up yours, Dad'. He continued his headlong flight and disappeared among the crowd on the opposite pavement.

This pedestrian behaved in a lunatic fashion, and the bread van driver was also at fault in following the Volvo too closely and too fast. The luckless Volvo driver was thus the victim of two other totally thoughtless road users.

Don't ever say there is no luck in driving; the gent in the Volvo would strongly disagree.

The best advice on pedestrian crossings is to treat them as if they were actual footpaths. Above all – **observation, anticipation, good manners *and* common sense**.

On the approach to a pedestrian crossing, make no mistake, the examiner will be watching you like a hawk, looking for just those qualities in your driving.

SECTION 20 OF THE TEST

A safe position for normal stops

On several occasions during your test the examiner will ask you to pull up by the kerb. His instruction will usually be 'I would like you to pull up in a convenient place on the left please'.

What does 'a convenient place' mean? Simple. It means convenient, safe, sensible and legal. Got that? Convenient, safe, sensible *and* legal.

Watch your fellow motorists, the ones who have passed their tests and should know better, but don't do as they do. Yellow lines, bus stops, pedestrian crossings – it's all the same to them. Their mission could be anything from doing a week's shopping to nipping across for a McDonalds' take-away.

The Highway Code gives a comprehensive list of places where one should avoid stopping. Rules 213–26 starting on page 55 cover the whole subject. Read and learn them, then read them again and think about each one. Think about why each of these is not a good or safe place to stop, they're just common sense.

On test, or at any time, the following guideline is best: don't park anywhere where it would cause danger or inconvenience to other road users.

You see we are back to the now familiar guidelines of good manners and common sense.

While on this subject it's worth just considering the sort of places where it would be unwise to **overtake**. If you think about it, these are much the same sort of places as the ones where you would not park.

Don't park anywhere where it would cause danger or inconvenience to other road users.

Do not, then, park or pull up, **except in an emergency**, in any position where you are breaking a traffic regulation or would be likely to endanger or inconvenience other road users, and this includes pedestrians.

In addition to asking you to pull up in a convenient place, the examiner may well ask you to pull up at a specific spot i.e. 'I want you to pull up by the next lamp post on the left', or 'level with the red pillar box on the left', or whatever.

This is a different matter, and in this case he is testing your ability to plan and control your slowing down and braking so that you come to a smooth standstill at a specific place.

Don't worry about the possibility that he might ask you to stop in an illegal place. An examiner will never set a trap for you in this fashion. He could, however, ask you to pull up at a convenient place when there are yellow lines, or zig-zag yellow 'school' lines beside the road. In this case he is not saying 'pull up here', he is asking you to pull up as soon as you come to an appropriate spot. You would therefore keep moving until you reached a convenient and legal place to stop.

Are you quite clear about these two different sets of instructions? The examiner will **never** direct you to do something illegal or dangerous, but he may well set you a little task which requires some thought and common sense.

It is most important that you listen carefully to the instructions given. The examiner will not chat to you or distract you, and will only speak to give you a specific instruction. If his intention is not clear, or you think you misheard him, do ask him to repeat the instruction, which he will gladly do. Make sure you understand him. Is he asking you to pull up in an appropriate place of your own choice, or is he directing you to stop in a specific location?

This choosing a safe place to stop simply calls for common sense and a knowledge of the relevant traffic signs and road markings. Common sense is everything in this section. Even after many years of teaching I am frequently filled with surprise and despair when I ask a pupil to pull up in a convenient place. Time and time again they stop on the left, right opposite the only vehicle in the whole street which is parked on the opposite side.

Yellow zig-zag school lines; I sometimes believe that drivers think these mark an area of outstanding architectural interest. Bus stops are another, and the much-used driveway to premises. Even the approach to pedestrian crossings is not exempt.

The mention of yellow lines at the side of the road is worth a few words. They seem to be widely misunderstood. Many drivers seem to think that double yellow lines are the same as single yellow lines, only more rigidly enforced. The popular belief is that you are more likely to get nicked on double yellow lines than on single ones.

I'm not going to slog through the regulations here, you should know the difference by now. If not, it's clearly explained in *The Highway Code*.

The subject was put into perspective recently by a lady who contributed a pithy little article to our local Institute of Advanced Motorists newsletter. She said that after a long spell of careful observation she had finally got this yellow lines business sussed out.

The meanings were now clear, she said. Single yellow lines mean that you can park with one pair of wheels on the footpath and double yellow lines mean you can park with both pairs of wheels on the footpath. Broken yellow lines however, mean that only broken vehicles may park on the footpath.

Your theory test could well ask you a question about single and double yellow lines. The above explanation is not recommended!

This section is one of the easiest of the lot to comply with, but it does claim its share of test failures. All it needs is knowledge of the rules of the game plus **observation** and **common sense**. So please, do use your brains, OK?

SECTION 21 OF THE TEST

Awareness of other road users

If we have just covered one of the easiest sections of the test, this Section 21 must be one of the most difficult with which to comply. I mean, '*anticipate the actions of other road users*'? Good grief, there's a lifetime's work in that sentence alone, and half of them would still be unpredictable. What are you supposed to be, for Heaven's sake – clairvoyant? I'm afraid, dear driver, that the answer to that question is a definite 'yes'.

There are now over 26 million vehicles in this country, and goodness knows how many bicycles and pedestrians. Sadly, any road user who is either thoughtless, ill-mannered, impatient, angry, careless, arrogant, selfish, stupid or just plain ignorant, could cause you to come unstuck on one or more of the many sections which we have analysed in this book, **unless**, that is, **unless you have seen the problem coming**, and often you can do just that.

Imagine a small boy on a bicycle just ahead, who does a rapid U-turn right in front of you, on spotting his friend on the other side of the road.

Imagine a lady, laden with shopping, who bolts across the road, right in front of you, attempting to catch a bus.

Imagine the driver in front of you signalling left, and then turning right.

Believe me, any one of these irresponsible road users could have failed you your test, and that might seem very unfair.

It is likely that the examiner would have anticipated these actions, and would have poised his feet over the dual controls, waiting to see whether or not you had seen the clues as to what was about to happen, as he had.

You don't need a crystal ball to forecast what is about to happen ahead of you. You need concentration, observation and an ability to anticipate the likely actions of others, and this anticipation, of course, is based on past experience.

We said earlier that it takes intelligence to drive well and safely. Without it you cannot interpret the many clues that other people give to their possible future behaviour. You will only pick up these clues if you are constantly on the alert for them. This is where the old saying falls down, that you can teach a monkey to drive if you've got enough bananas. You might train some amiable primate to get into gear and move off, but would he deduce anything from the reversing lights on the stationary car just ahead? I doubt it. (Never considered bananas for pupils before. Might be worth considering).

When driving, you must look much further ahead than when walking. Most of the time you need to be looking ahead to where you are going to be in five or six seconds time, and that could be as much as the length of a football pitch; much further at motorway speeds.

Look suspiciously at the pedestrian who begins to run. Look at **any youngster** on a bike; give **cyclists room**. A learned judge recently ruled that 'a cyclist is entitled to his wobble'. A very sensible statement. Give **any cyclist** room for a wobble, and the younger they are, the more carefully you approach them.

Look suspiciously at the driver in front if he is having an animated discussion with the passenger, and gesticulating in the process. They do not have their minds on their driving, and are usually about to do something foolish with little or no warning. Nowadays they could even be on the telephone, with little concentration on the driving, although this is now illegal.

This section is essentially about using your powers of observation and deduction, and letting the examiner see that you are looking both ahead and behind at what other people are doing, thinking about what they might do next and when they are likely to do it.

The examiner will only use this section as a basis for faulting you if your error cannot be classified under one of the previous sections. For example, if you emerge at a junction and fail to see and allow for a cyclist, he will not fault you for not being aware of or anticipating the cyclist. That would indeed be relevant to this present section, but you would be marked under section 15 of the test, *'act properly at road junctions with regard to observation'.*

This current section, 21, is often overlooked because it is difficult to define, and seems to call for no clearly prescribed action. It is probably one of the most difficult sections with which to comply and it is certainly the one which separates the experienced driver from the beginner, the expert from the novice.

All the smooth gear changes, accurate steering and smooth braking, all this car handling expertise will be useless to you unless you can develop the art of looking ahead, looking for little clues to other people's possible actions. You must develop a gut feeling for what is happening about you, and for what is likely to happen as a consequence.

This flair for intelligent anticipation is not just done for the examiner's benefit. It is the very essence of survival in all your future driving. How can you be in the right place on the road at the right time at the right speed and in the right gear unless you have given thought to what is likely to happen next?

Being *'aware of and anticipating the actions of other road users'* means covering all those potential situations for which there is no precise rule. If there were rules or guidelines for every possible, conceivable traffic situation, then *The Highway Code* would be thicker than the Bible and virtually impossible to take in. It must all depend, therefore, on your **awareness**, **observation** and your **intelligent anticipation** based on what you have observed, and your knowledge of the rules of the game.

The final contribution to this anticipation thing is **experience**, and that is what makes this section so hard to go along with, because at this point you haven't got much experience.

What is experience then? Well, it is the accumulated wisdom which is based on earlier mistakes – yours and other people's. It is a wise driver who profits from previous mistakes, previous happenings. It is a wise driver who, with perhaps a million miles behind him, will tell you he is still learning. That is experience, and that is why it is difficult to accurately anticipate other road users' actions and reactions when you haven't been using the road for long.

Think about what this section of the test requires of you; it's a bit vague, hard to define, but it's so important. You want it in two words? **COMMON SENSE.**

SECTION 22 OF THE TEST

Use of ancillary controls

I heard recently of a lady who turned up for her test, accompanied by her instructor. It was already raining. When she moved off from the test centre with the examiner, she switched on the ignition and the windscreen wipers operated immediately, because they had been in use when she arrived with her instructor and switched the engine off.

Ten minutes into the test it stopped raining and the sun came out, but the windscreen wipers plodded gamely on, squawking away on the dry glass, which tends to both wear out the rubber wiper blades and scratch the windscreen. The examiner was eventually moved to say, 'Might we not have the wipers switched off?'

'How does one do that?' enquired this good lady, and the examiner was not impressed. Apart from anything else, it was her own car!

Since July 1996 *The Highway Code* quiz has been dropped from the practical test, being now well covered by the theory test. In its place we have a new section 22 of the practical test – knowledge of the ancillary controls.

Even if you are in the dual-controlled car belonging to your instructor, you must know how to operate all the minor controls, (the main controls being accelerator, footbrake, clutch, steering wheel, handbrake and gear lever).

When you return to the test centre, your test drive completed, the examiner may ask you to show him how to operate some of the minor controls. These can include horn, sidelights, headlights, high-intensity rear fog lights, front windscreen wipers and washers, rear window wipers and washers, front and rear window demisting systems, the car ventilating system, bonnet lock, fuel filler cap, direction indicators, dip/main beam headlight switch, hazard warning lights, door locks and so on.

If he asks you to demonstrate the headlight dipswitch and you squirt water all over the windscreen, which drips through the open window onto his trousers, he will not be well suited. Similarly, if you produce Radio Humberside instead of the hazard warning lights, there are no brownie points in this either.

Your instructor should make quite sure, early on in your course of lessons, that you are thoroughly familiar with all these minor controls. Many of them are often needed quite quickly.

The unfortunate lady we have just been discussing, was not entirely to blame for being ignorant of how to switch off the windscreen wipers, but her instructor certainly was.

Whatever car you drive – your instructor's, your parents, your own – you **must** be shown how to operate all the minor controls. They may be minor but it is certainly not enough to know how to start and stop and steer. You must know how to give a warning flash of your headlights, demist your rear window or use any of these controls at short notice. It may make the difference between avoiding an accident or having one.

Don't overlook this very important final section.

A final word on minor controls – 'gadgets' and I'm talking about **MOBILE PHONES**. You've all got mobile phones. Yes you have – I've seen them.

Do NOT take it on test, but if you must have it with you, **switch it off first**.

When you have passed your test, don't drive and talk on the telephone. I know a lot of people do so, and they are often driving very badly. Apart from putting their own and other people's safety at risk, **they are breaking the law**.

Prior to December 2003 there was no specific offence of using a mobile phone while driving, although you could be prosecuted for doing so, and many drivers were. The offence they were charged with was 'not being in full control of the vehicle'.

Since December 1st 2003, however, using a mobile phone while driving (except a 'hands free' phone) has been a specific offence, which can carry a hefty fine, **so don't do it**.

THE GREAT DAY – THE TEST

Your instructor will tell you when to apply for a test, and he will base his advice on the stage you have reached, coupled with the waiting time at your local test centre. If he believes you are not yet ready to take and pass the test, he will advise you against applying for it.

If you disregard his advice and still apply, your instructor would be quite within his rights if he declined to let you take the test in the driving school car. If he advises you to delay your application for a while, he is not trying to squeeze more money out of you, he is trying to stop you wasting money by taking the test prematurely and failing. Do take your instructor's guidance in this matter.

So you have applied, you have received your appointment card and the day arrives. **Panic!** The thing to ask yourself is 'Has the examiner lain awake all night worrying about meeting me? Will he at this very moment be biting his nails, dying to go to the loo, his tongue sticking to the roof of his mouth?' The answer, of course, is no he won't. To him your test is just another routine drive round the town. You should treat it as exactly that, and when you actually set off, just concentrate on what you are doing, not on your passenger. This is simply an opportunity to demonstrate to a complete stranger just how well you can do the job.

Your instructor should have given you several mock tests in which he recreates for you the exact manner in which the real thing is conducted. The actual result of your mock test is not nearly so important as the fact that you have had an opportunity to experience what it actually feels like to drive alone, for about 40 minutes.

You really are on your own on your test. The examiner will not help you or encourage you, nor will he criticise you while you are driving. He will only speak to you in order to give you directions as to the route you are to follow, or to ask you to pull up in some convenient place.

This silence is not because he is in a foul mood, or doesn't like the look of you. His purpose in testing you is to assess your ability to cope alone with whatever traffic situations you might meet, so for this reason he does his best to pretend he isn't there.

By far the best course for you is to go along with this. Imagine that you've passed your test and now you really are driving alone. If you then come to some situation which needs a bit of thought, don't approach it on the basis of 'oh help, what does he expect me to do here?' Just think 'now how do I tackle this?' or 'what would my instructor expect me to do here?'

A couple of mock tests should have made you confidently aware of exactly what the simple test process involves. The only unknown factors are your route, and what you will meet as you follow it. By now, however, you will have reached a standard which will enable you to take all normal traffic situations and hazards confidently in your stride.

Pupils have repeatedly made two observations following their tests. One is how quickly the time seems to go while on test, and the other comforting factor is that no matter how dry-mouthed and uptight you might be as the actual test time draws nearer, once you have set off with the examiner aboard and you are doing something familiar, then the test nerves and the colliwobbles seem to disappear. I always tell pupils this, and no-one ever believes it, but when they get back from the drive, they confirm that this is what actually happened.

After all, what is the very worst that can happen? You could fail, but it isn't the end of the world. It's disappointing, it's a blow to the ego, and it's going to cost a bit more money. Nothing actually happens though. The man isn't going to eat you. He simply says, 'I'm sorry Mr Witherspoon, but you haven't reached the required standard today. Now these are the points you will have to concentrate on.'

He will then briefly run over the point or points which failed you.

He will give you a copy of his marking sheet on which are listed all the 22 points in the test syllabus. He will have marked a / against any item on which you earned a major fault, and it will either be in the 'S' for serious or the 'D' for dangerous columns. You will also see a / marked for each minor fault in the first column. The minor faults in each section are added up, the totals marked in the next column.

See the copy of the marking sheet on page 29.

Failure is what you have been dreading, but if it happens, it's almost an anti-climax. If failure had meant having to run naked through the market place with a notice round your neck saying 'I've just blown my driving test', then there would be some reason for anxiety beforehand. All that happens, though, is that the examiner says 'I'm sorry, but not today. Better luck next time'. Then he pushes off to make a cup of tea.

Is that really worth all that loss of sleep?

Why do candidates get themselves in such a state on test day? It's not the most vital interview you ever attended, it's not the first night of your honeymoon – it's another drive round the town with a polite and, usually, sympathetic passenger. The less uptight you are, the better you will be able to concentrate calmly and logically on what you're doing. So think about it.

Taking the 22 separate sections of the test, with all their various sub-sections, there are over 40 different headings under which you can come unstuck, so you see there is plenty of scope for failure. We have gone through all these 40 or so hurdles in this book, but it doesn't mean you are some sort of total dunce if you are human enough to trip over some of them.

There is one very real crumb of comfort for those who don't pass first time. When you do pass, at the second or maybe the third attempt, make no mistake about it, you are going to be a better driver then than you were when you took your first test. I have never known a second or third time pass where this assurance did not hold good.

One word of caution at this point: don't turn up for your test solemnly swearing, through clenched teeth, 'I've got to pass today, I simply must pass today'.

I have often noticed that the I-must-pass-today brigade usually fail. It is quite possible to try too hard, to the point where all contact with reality seems to be lost. Just decide that you are going to do your best, you are going to think about what you're doing, and above all, relax. Remember **good manners** and **common sense**. Most important, enjoy the drive. You are literally putting a new-found skill to the test; you like driving or you wouldn't be there, so enjoy it.

Turn up in the right frame of mind then; your instructor will help you here. He's a bit of a psychologist you know –he has to be to do his job well. He will no doubt give you a final short lesson just prior to the test in order to iron out any small last-minute worries.

The test is not a wake or a wedding, or any sort of function where high fashion is of any importance. Do wear sensible, comfortable clothes, particularly shoes which are comfortable to drive in.

We know that your colour, creed or appearance have no bearing on the result of the test; only the driving matters. I have always felt, however, that if you turn up looking like a total menace to society, the examiner is going to see you, if only subconsciously, as a bit 'iffy' before you have even started. I therefore try to get my pupils to the test looking like reasonably normal citizens.

I well remember Roland, a young man who had grown up in a very restricted, almost Quaker-like atmosphere at home. He ultimately rebelled, and would go about the town with a Mohican haircut, and his earlobes full of assorted ironmongery. His backside hung out of a pair of truly disgusting jeans, held together at the knees with large safety pins.

You would not have let your daughter within miles of Roland. For all that, he was a courteous, thoughtful chap, and moreover a good, sensible driver. He did not give the visual impression of any of these qualities, however; he just looked horrible. I suggested, as tactfully as possible, that he might do something about his image on test day, and he did me proud.

There was no denying the haircut, but the rest was eminently presentable. Gone were all the earrings, only the perforations showed where they'd been. He passed his test, as I was confident he would. The examiner actually complimented me on a very good drive by Roland. I like to think the modified appearance helped a bit to keep the examiner in an open frame of mind.

I cannot recall Roland without bringing Ruby Higgins vividly to mind. Some pupils fade into the mists of time, some you remember.

I remember Ruby.

Ruby was definitely unique, and well built with it. One week her hair would be green, the next lesson it could be pink, and styled to resemble an explosion in a mattress factory. She had an extensive wardrobe, appearing sometimes as a fully paid up dolly-bopper, the next week looking like an Albanian goatherd – a bit like Roland.

Like Roland, her earlobes were weighed down by assorted metal work. As test day loomed nearer I steered the subject delicately round to image and first impressions. After that I could only wait and hope.

I picked Ruby up an hour before her test. It was a hot day in July, and she had dressed accordingly. She had on a very tight denim micro skirt, which just about covered her credentials. Way below this were a pair of dazzling white boots, and the only other visible garment was a sort of wide mesh string vest. Panoramic views of Ruby were visible through the string vest, and the overall effect was, to say the least, riveting.

I pondered apprehensively on the effect Ruby might have on HM Department for Transport and its appointed officials.

We had a very good, well-driven hour's rehearsal and made for the test centre at the appointed time. As with thousands before her, Ruby's confidence was waning and her anxiety growing.

In our rather claustrophobic waiting room, Ruby stood, one hand on the table, nervously licking her lips and, almost imperceptibly, gyrating her pelvis; something she tended to do, I think, quite unconsciously. Bang on 10.30, the examiners trooped in, led by our Mr Webster, crying a cheerful 'good morning' to those assembled. His eye lit upon Ruby and he lurched to a standstill – gobsmacked.

He cleared his throat. 'Miss Higgins?' he croaked.

Since every other occupant of the waiting room was male, this struck me as something of a rhetorical question.

The form was signed, driving licence produced and checked, and Ruby was hoarsely invited to lead the way out to her vehicle. They set off, Mr Webster following, apparently wracked by a spasm of uncontrollable coughing, his eyes fixed firmly on Ruby's undulating bum.

She passed, and the point is that, notwithstanding the boots, the bum and the vest, Ruby was a capable driver with a natural aptitude for handling a vehicle, plus a good traffic sense, and she had obviously got her act together for the occasion. She deserved to pass, but I sometimes think of that particular day and wonder what actually clinched it.

I saw her a couple of months later, driving a beat-up old Mini, handpainted bright pink – the Mini, not Ruby. The back end of the exhaust was attached to the car with bailer twine. Not for Ruby the pathetic and puerile window stickers with messages like 'My other car is a Ferrari' or 'I love Milton Keynes'. No, Ruby's single sticker, on the boot lid, was of a more philosophical nature and bore the rather poignant legend: 'Sex is like air, only important when you're not getting any'.

Like Ruby, I thought, this at least was original. She was driving sensibly, and looked well content. Yes, I do indeed remember Ruby.

When young pupils ask me what to wear for the test, I think, on balance that Roland's approach is the best. So just look neat

'Sex is like air, only important when you're not getting any'!

and tidy, and wear things that are both practical and comfortable.

A little hint on 'mirror'. Before you set off on your test drive, the examiner will do his best to put you at ease while he gives you your short briefing. This simply consists of him telling you that he wants you, at all junctions, to follow the road straight ahead unless he tells you otherwise, *or unless traffic signs tell you otherwise*. Don't overlook that phrase, and be careful to look for signs like this

  or this –

or indeed any other mandatory sign which warns you of a necessary change of direction.

So then, while you are driving, the examiner is only going to speak to you to say one of three things. Either 'take the next turning to the left please', or 'take the next turning to the right', or 'will you pull up at a convenient place on the left?'

In other words, all he is going to say is 'turn left', 'turn right', or 'stop'. Now, you know that you cannot do any of these without a look in the mirror, so it follows that whenever you hear his voice – **mirror**.

Don't forget though, that you will need to check your mirror on many occasions when he hasn't spoken. Any hazard ahead of you such as a parked vehicle, a cyclist, or anything which makes you alter either your speed or course, any of these means a mirror check first. Although he may look half asleep, don't be misled, he will probably have seen the hazard before you do, and he will be quietly observing you, waiting for that mirror check.

Let's just go back to his giving directions. Note that there is a difference between 'take the next road on the left' and 'at the supermarket turn left'.

Many a test has been failed through failing to spot this difference. If the command is 'take the next road on the left', you can check your mirror and fairly safely put on your left signal. If, however, the command is 'at the supermarket turn left', then immediately check the mirror by all means, but *don't* immediately switch on the signal. First make quite sure that there is not another turning to the left before the point where he wants you to turn. You could so easily collect a fault for signalling incorrectly; in this case too soon.

Don't forget, there are no different levels of passing or failing. There are no honours or distinctions, and no 'almost passed'. If you miss out a vital mirror check you fail just as certainly as if you had hit a bus as you drove the wrong way down a one-way street.

If you think you have made an error, then take care not to repeat it. Don't dwell on it however. Don't spend the next five minutes mentally kicking yourself – you won't be able to concentrate on what you are doing *now*. You haven't failed until the examiner tells you so, and that won't be until you have arrived back at the test centre, so don't give up half way through. Try to be relaxed; allowing yourself to be put under pressure doesn't help at all.

We could write a separate book of test hints, most of them useless. Don't be put off or influenced by know-all colleagues. 'Mr Scrooge is horrible, you want the other one, with the curly hair.' 'You'll never pass on a Friday afternoon.'

Forget it, it's all rubbish, mostly put about by candidates who have failed, and who need a good excuse for having done so.

If you get your act together, as you have so often done on lessons, and keep it together for just over half an hour, then you've cracked it. Be calm. Act normally.

Drive normally. You must be in the right place on the road at the right time, at the right speed for the conditions, and in the right gear for that speed. Your driving must always reflect good manners and common sense. You approach all hazards with the mirror, signal, position, speed and gear routine.

That sums up good driving in three sentences.

Finally, the importance of *The Highway Code* and *The Driving Test* cannot be overstressed. Get to know them inside out. If you know what they mean and do as they say, you'll pass, no doubt of it.

Do please note that before the examiner can start the test you must produce for him both the plastic and paper parts of your provisional driving licence, plus your theory test and hazard perception test pass certificates. Without these items, the test cannot proceed.

Good luck, because luck is also an essential ingredient.

You must be in the right place on the road at the right time, at the right speed for the conditions, and in the right gear for that speed. Your driving must always reflect good manners and common sense. You approach all hazards with the mirror, signal, position, speed and gear routine.

THE THEORY AND HAZARD PERCEPTION TEST

Theory Test

This book is essentially about the practical aspects of the driving test, but it would be incomplete without a passing mention of the theory test.

Having waded through 160 odd pages about the practical test, touching on the theory test now is rather like putting the cart before the horse, because you need to pass the theory test before taking the practical driving test.

The enlarged 1999 and subsequent editions of *The Highway Code* contain all the information needed to pass the theory test, and *The Complete Theory Test for Cars and Motorcycles'* is a definitive guide. Produced by the Publications Unit of the Driving Standards Agency and published by The Stationery Office, is available from all good bookshops, and can also be had as a CD-ROM. It's the best ten quid's worth I have seen for a long while.

It covers the theory test in great detail, it lists all the questions you may be asked, and not only does it give all the correct answers but explains why the correct answer **IS** the correct answer. As a learning tool therefore, it supplements to a considerable degree the wide range of facts and theories on driving lore which you absorb as part of your practical driving lessons.

The theory test is a multiple-choice test containing 35 questions and is done on a 'touch screen' television screen. To pass you must give a minimum of 30 correct answers.

The subject matter is divided into 14 sections, as follows:-

1. Alertness
2. Attitude
3. Safety and your vehicle
4. Safety margins
5. Hazard awareness
6. Vulnerable road users
7. Other types of vehicle
8. Vehicle handling
9. Motorway rules
10. Rules of the road
11. Road and traffic signs
12. Documents
13. Accidents
14. Vehicle loading

These 14 sections are listed in *The Complete Theory Test for Cars and Motorcycles*, and enlarged on in some detail. Even if there were no theory test, this book would still be a really invaluable guide for the learner driver, taking him way beyond the boundaries of the basic practical driving test.

Although you must pass the theory test before taking the practical, my advice would be not to sit the theory test before starting your course of driving lessons.

Theory tests tend to have a much shorter waiting time than the practical tests, so get well into your practical course before applying for a theory test. This will enable you to gain experience of the use of the road and handling a vehicle, and this experience will make it much easier to understand and absorb the contents of the theory test syllabus.

The theory test is not difficult, provided you have done your homework. The multiple choice questions often offer two or three really daft answers and one common sense answer – other answers are not so obvious. I can only stress again that if you have really soaked up *The Highway Code* and the *Complete Theory Test book*, you will pass easily. If you cannot achieve a pass in the theory test, then you are certainly not ready to drive solo on the Queen's highway.

Finally, try to do better than the candidate who features in what is undoubtedly an apocryphal story. It is rumoured that on coming to the question which said 'what is the commonest road sign in Great Britain', this character wrote 'Pick your own Strawberries'.

Hazard Perception Test

Many inexperienced drivers are involved in accidents, often because they are not used to recognising a potentially dangerous situation ahead until it's too late to take avoiding action.

For this reason, the DSA introduced the Hazard Perception Test in November 2002. Briefly, this calls for the candidate to watch 14 short video clips of traffic situations. In these 14 clips are a total of 15 DEVELOPING hazards. The buzz word is **developing**, and on seeing a potential hazard developing, the candidate clicks the mouse.

Everything is a hazard – a telegraph pole is a hazard because you might bump into it. Similarly a car parked, half on the footpath, is a potential hazard, but if you clicked for this, you would score no points. If this parked car switched on a right indicator, then here is a DEVELOPING hazard, and a click here would score 5 points. If it then started to pull out, a click would only earn you 3 or 4 points, because you missed the first clue. if you only clicked when the car had emerged onto the road and was gathering speed, then you would score zero – you're too late. Repeatedly clicking for no good reason will lose points, remember, you're looking for a developing hazard, not just anything that might look a bit iffy.

The DSA handout says 'a driver skilled in hazard perception could be expected to click 10 or 12 times during one clip'. Maximum possible score is 75 points, and pass mark for car/motor cycle learners is 44. The hazard perception test is taken at the same time as the theory test. You can swot up for the theory test, but not for the HPT, it's intelligent observation, and you need to be alert, (oh yes, your country needs lerts!!!).

WHERE DO I GO FROM HERE? – IAM? – PASS PLUS?

So you passed? Well congratulations. That ought to be the end of the book then, but I would like to offer a few words of advice about what comes next. Yes, I suppose it's a bit of a sermon, but what did you expect?

This is not the end of learning to drive, it's where it really begins. What you have achieved is a good grounding in the art, and you have qualified to go solo – that's all. You are not yet up to Police Class 1 standard, nor are you Michael Schumacher.

Your first drive by yourself is a milestone in your motoring life. Don't attempt too much on the first outing, don't go straight into the middle of Birmingham on a Saturday morning, and certainly you should not go for a good old thrash up the motorway.

Where motorways are concerned it's a whole new ball game. Things happen a great deal more quickly on a motor way, and a great deal more inevitably. It is a very different experience. If there is a motorway within reasonable reach of you, get your instructor to take you for at least two more lessons, and introduce you to motorway driving properly. He will be more than pleased to do so. It is the only sensible thing to do.

We have a truly ridiculous situation in the UK, unlike many continental countries. Here, learner drivers are not allowed on motorways, and so they are turned out, allegedly as fully qualified drivers, but with no motorway know how other than a couple of motorway questions from *The Highway Code*. We are now addressing this problem with the 'Pass Plus' scheme.

Despite modern roads, safer vehicles and constant legislation, we are still killing around 3.5 thousand human beings every year on British roads. This is about one every two-and-a-half hours, seven days a week. Increasing new legislation is aimed at addressing this awful state of affairs, but sadly, one of the prime causes cannot be controlled by legislation. We're talking about **attitude**. It is impossible to govern people's attitude by laws – their attitude towards other road users and road safety generally. You can't **make** drivers practise good manners or common sense.

Please don't think something like 'I've passed my test, I can forget all that boring twaddle I got from my stuffy instructor and the po-faced examiner, from here on I can do things my way'.

This is sadly an all too common attitude and leads inevitably to bad driving and a greatly increased risk of accidents. Don't drive as you see so many others do. Drive the way you've been taught, and to the standard that got you through your test.

Don't think that all bad examples come from boy racers in hotted-up Escorts. The executive in his expensive company car can be seen any day of the week doing the most stupid things. Waiting in a traffic queue near a level crossing, with his car actually astride the railway line, with never a thought as to what might happen if the gates closed. Doing 80 mph down the motorway, 10 metres or so from the vehicle in front, while actually on the telephone to his office. Doing the same 80 mph down the same motorway in heavy rain, with no lights on at all; the list is endless, and yet any of these pieces of folly would have failed him his basic driving test. Common sense?

When you actually get your first car it is a wonderful moment, whether it is brand new or has 70,000 miles on the clock.

Do resist the temptation to hang furry dice from the mirror, they are a dangerous distraction. Don't have fluffy animals climbing up the windows, the windows are for seeing through. Make no mistake, when you see a car festooned with all this infantile junk, it serves only one useful purpose. It tells you quite reliably that the driver concerned has got a mental age of about nine, and is probably going to do something stupid fairly soon.

So then, concentrate on improving your driving. There is no such person as the perfect driver, but you can derive a lot of satisfaction from working towards that goal.

If you really have a feeling for driving and enjoy and take a pride in your new found skill, you might like to think about upgrading your qualifications. When you have driven for a while, and have some miles behind you, you might consider taking a more advanced test. This can be done with the IAM (the Institute of Advanced Motorists). The IAM have local groups all over the country. Joining the local group as an associate member is the first step. The full members of the group, i.e. those who have passed their advanced test, will willingly give you guidance and advice to bring you up to advanced standard, and this guidance is, of course, free.

The Institute of Advanced Motorists are at
   IAM House, 510 Chiswick High Road
   LONDON W4 5RG. Telephone 0208 996 9600.

A phone call (24 hour service) will bring you a note of the name and address of the secretary of the group nearest to your home.

The Royal Society for the Prevention of Accidents (RoSPA) also offer an advanced driving qualification, as do the Driving Instructors Association (DIA).

This last one is the DIAmond advanced driving qualification, and coaching for this can be had from any DIA instructor.

All three organisations work towards the same end – raising the standard of the keen and conscientious driver to an above average level, a level which carries a respected and widely recognised qualification.

You cannot take your IAM advanced test until you have held a full licence for six months, but in the meantime you can take advantage of the best thing that's happened to new drivers for years. It's called 'Pass Plus', and I want to use the last couple of pages of the book to give you the details. It's the last and probably the best bit of advice I have to offer.

It came about because for some time motor insurance companies have been paying out huge sums in injury, death and accident claims arising from traffic accidents involving newly qualified drivers. As a result, newly qualified drivers are having to pay extremely high insurance premiums on their first car.

The alarming facts are these:-

1. Newly qualified drivers account for about 10 per cent of all drivers on the roads;
2. They are involved in over 20 per cent of all road accidents;
3. They are involved in 25 per cent of all fatal accidents;

What does that tell us? Precisely.

The major insurance companies have got together with the Driving Standards Agency and devised a simple six-part extension to the syllabus for the learner test.

The six extra subjects covered are:

1. Rural road driving (there are more serious accidents on narrow, twisty country lanes than you would imagine);
2. City centre driving;
3. Bad weather driving;
4. Night driving;
5. Fast dual-carriageway driving;
6. Motorway driving.

We said earlier that we are almost alone in Europe in not allowing **learner** drivers onto motorways, but we allow people to go alone, half an hour after passing their test, straight onto a busy motorway with no previous experience at all. This in my view is a bad loophole which the 'Pass Plus' scheme now addresses.

These important six subjects can be covered, after passing your practical test, with a Pass Plus Registered Instructor. There is no extra test to take, but when the instructor reports to the DSA that you have satisfactorily completed the short course, you receive a certificate to this effect from the DSA.

Here's where the bonus comes in. This certificate is recognised by a high proportion of reputable insurance companies and brokers and will qualify you for a significant reduction in the cost of your first insurance premium. Your Pass Plus instructor will have an up-to-date list of participating insurers. The saving on the cost of the premium usually more than covers the cost of the extra six lessons. Even without the financial incentive, the scheme makes a lot of sense.

The six subjects are all vital to your future safe driving, and the motorway section is absolutely invaluable.

Pass Plus is currently entirely voluntary, but I would like to see its syllabus become mandatory. Maybe it will one day. It would certainly save a lot of lives.

So let me leave you with one more definition, a definition of road safety: Road safety is your ever-present awareness of your responsibility for the safety of others.

Go safely then, and enjoy your driving.

Road safety is your ever-present awareness of your responsibility for the safety of others.